Workbook I

The Influential Manager

Manage People
Certificate
S/NVQ Level 4

Institute of Management Open Learning Programme

Series editor: Gareth Lewis
Author: Lisa Davis

the Institute
of Management

Pergamon
Flexible
Learning

Pergamon Flexible Learning
An imprint of Butterworth-Heinemann
Linacre House, Jordan Hill, Oxford OX2 8DP
225 Wildwood Avenue, Woburn, MA 01801-2041
A division of Reed Educational and Professional Publishing Ltd

℞ A member of the Reed Elsevier plc group

OXFORD   AUCKLAND   BOSTON
JOHANNESBURG   MELBOURNE   NEW DELHI

First published 1997
Reprinted 1998, 1999, 2000

British Library Cataloguing in Publication Data
A catalogue record for this book is available from the British Library

ISBN 0 7506 3662 9

Typeset by Avocet Typeset, Brill, Aylesbury, Bucks
Printed and bound in Great Britain

FOR EVERY TITLE THAT WE PUBLISH, BUTTERWORTH-HEINEMANN
WILL PAY FOR BTCV TO PLANT AND CARE FOR A TREE.

Contents

Series overview

The Institute of Management Open Learning Programme is a series of workbooks prepared by the Institute of Management and Pergamon Open Learning for managers seeking to develop themselves.

Comprising seventeen open learning workbooks, the programme covers the best of modern management theory and practice, and each workbook provides a range of frameworks and techniques to improve your effectiveness as a manager, thus helping you acquire the knowledge and skill to make you fully competent in your role.

Each workbook is written by an experienced management writer and covers an important management topic or theme. The activities both reinforce learning and help to relate the generic ideas to your individual work context. While coverage of each topic is fully comprehensive, additional reading suggestions and reference sources are given for those who wish to study to a greater depth.

Designed to be practical, stimulating and challenging, the aim of the workbooks is to improve performance at work by benefiting you and your organization. This practical focus is at the heart of the competence based approach that has been adopted by the programme.

The structure of the programme

The design and overall structure of the programme has two main organizing principles, both of which are closely linked to the national standards for management developed by the MCI (Management Charter Initiative).

First, the workbooks are grouped according to the key roles of management.

- Underpinning the management standards are a series of **personal competences** which describe the personal skills required by all managers, which are essential to skill in all the main functional or key role areas.
- **Manage Activities** describes the principles of managing processes and activities, with service to the customer as an essential part of this.
- **Manage Resources** describes the acquisition, control and monitoring of financial and other resources.
- **Manage People** looks at the key skills involved in leadership, developing one's staff and managing their performance.

■ **Manage Information** discusses the acquisition, storage and use of information for communication, problem solving and decision making.

In addition, there are three specialized key roles: **Manage Quality, Manage Projects** and **Manage Energy**. The workbooks cover the first two of these. Unlike the four primary key roles above, these are not compulsory for certificate, diploma or S/NVQ requirements, but provide options for the latter.

Together, these key roles provide a comprehensive description of the fundamental principles of management as it applies in any organization – commercial, maintained sector or not-for-profit.

Second, the programme is organized according to **levels of management**, seniority and responsibility.

Level 4 represents first line management. In accredited programmes this is equivalent to S/NVQ Level 4, Certificate in Management or CMS. Level 5 is equivalent to middle/senior management and is accredited at S/NVQ Level 5, Diploma in Management or DMS. There are two S/NVQs at Level 5: Operational Management and Strategic Management. The operations role is focussed internally within an organization on the maintenance of systems and standards of output, whilst the strategic role is focussed on the whole organization, including the external operating environment, and looks at setting directions.

Together, the workbooks cover all the background knowledge you need to have for all units of competence in the MCI standards at Level 4 and Level 5 (apart from the specialized units in the key role Manage Energy). They also provide skills development and opportunities for portfolio building.

For a comprehensive list of workbooks, see page ix. For a comprehensive list of links with the standards, see the *User Guide*.

How to use the programme

The programme is deliberately designed to be flexible and can be used in a variety of ways:

■ to update on important management topics and themes, or develop individual skills: as the workbooks are grouped according to themes, it should be easy for you to pick out one that suits your needs

■ as part of generic management development programmes: you can choose the modules that fit the themes of the programme

■ as part of, and in support of, accredited competence-based programmes.

For N/SVQs at both Levels 4 and 5, there are options in the combinations of units that make up the various awards. By using the map provided in the *User Guide*, individuals will be able to select the workbooks appropriate to their specific needs, and their chosen accreditation options. Some of the activities will help you provide evidence for your portfolio; where we think this is the case, we give the relevant reference to the standards.

For Certificate or CMS, Diploma or DMS, individuals should choose modules that not only meet their individual needs but also satisfy the requirements of the delivering body and the awarding body.

You may need help and guidance in these choices, and the *User Guide* sets out the options and advice in much more detail. A fuller description of the potential uses of this material in evidence gathering and portfolio building can also be found in the *User Guide*, as can a detailed description of the contents of each workbook.

Workbooks in the Institute of Management Open Learning Programme

Manage People (Level 5)

14 *The New Model Leader*

Manage Information (Level 4)

15 *Making Rational Decisions*
16 *Communication*

Manage Information (Level 5)

17 *Successful Information Management*

Manage Quality (Level 4)

3 *Understanding Business Process Management**
4 *Customer Focus**

Manage Quality (Level 5)

5 *Getting TQM to Work**

Manage Projects (Level 4)

8 *Project Management**

Manage Projects (Level 5)

8 *Project Management**

Support Materials

18 *User Guide*
19 *Mentor Guide*

An asterisk indicates that a particular workbook also contains material suitable for a particular key role or personal competence.

Links to qualifications

S/NVQ programmes

This workbook can help candidates to achieve credit and develop skills in the key role of managing people and covers the following units and elements:

C2   Develop your own resources
C2.1 Develop yourself to improve your performance
C2.2 Manage your time and resources to meet objectives
C3   Enhance your own performance
C3.1 Continuously develop your own knowledge and skills
C3.2 Optimize your own resources to meet your objectives
C6.3 Provide guidance on values at work

Certificate and Diploma programmes

This Workbook, together with the other workbooks on managing people (2 – *Managing Yourself*, 11 – *Getting the Right People to do the Right Job*, 12 – *Developing Yourself and Your Staff*, 13 – *Building a High Performance Team* and 14 – *The New Model Leader*), covers all of the knowledge required in the key role Manage People for Certificate in Management and CMS programmes, as well as Diploma in Management and DMS programmes.

Links to other workbooks

This is one of two workbooks – the other being 2, *Managing Yourself* – which cover the units of the S/NVQ which are common to both levels.

Related workbooks are found in Module 4, Manage People, and (at Level 4) are:

11 *Getting the Right People to do the Right Job*
12 *Developing Yourself and Your Staff*
13 *Building a High Performance Team*

and at Level 5:

14 *The New Model Leader*

The theme of this workbook is closely associated with:

16 *Communication*

Introduction

Many management books talk about empowering *your staff* or *the workforce*, but in this Workbook we will be focusing on the skills and techniques which will empower *you*, as a manager.

Management isn't always easy. Being a manager involves a whole host of tasks – from taking care of people and resources through to initiating new projects, keeping a watchful eye on productivity and lots, lots more. New managers, who move up from a team-leading or supervisory role, are often shocked to discover the level of managerial responsibility which comes with the territory. Managers working in any kind of organization need a wide range of skills and techniques to cope with regular, everyday activities, new and highly demanding activities and, of course, the dramas which are, for most people, a regular feature of managerial life.

Many managers stumble from crisis to crisis and reluctantly accept *fire-fighting,* on a daily basis, as part of the job. These people tend not to work efficiently or effectively because, generally, they are too busy dashing from here to there and back again, trying to solve problems and put out fires. The difference between this kind of manager and the kind of manager who plans ahead, thinks things through and focuses on outcomes is *empowerment.*

Empowerment is about knowing what you want to achieve and what you have to do to achieve it, doing it, and then getting the right results. Empowered managers have a working knowledge of a range of tools and techniques which allow them to approach their tasks and responsibilities with confidence. Empowered managers may not get **everything** right **all of the time** (no-one does), but they do have the necessary skills to enable them to:

- choose where they are going
- plan how they are going to get there
- judge whether or not they have arrived

Empowered managers also use past experience as a basis for current decisions, and transfer current learning into the future so that they can avoid making the same mistake twice.

In this Workbook we shall be looking at ways in which you can empower yourself to work ethically, plan and prioritize objectives, influence other people and make decisions. These are four key management skills and will help you to tackle a wide range of management tasks confidently and with a high degree of personal effectiveness.

Objectives

By the end of this Workbook you should be able to:

- Understand and adopt an ethical approach to management issues which is both open and reasoned
- Plan and prioritize objectives
- Apply techniques to influence and communicate with colleagues
- Understand techniques for decision making

Section 1 Ethics at work

Introduction

As Sir Peter Parker KBE, LVO, CIMgt says in his foreword to *Walking the Tightrope*[1]

Business is no longer just about the bottom line – there is now a top line for top management. Organizations are having to widen their vision to include social values and environmental issues, as well as ethical and moral principles.

Shareholders and consumers are beginning to demand an ethical approach to making money, and companies who are not prepared to meet those demands risk losing market share and credibility. For most managers, working in most organizations, this means having to look carefully not only at productivity and profit, but at the way in which that productivity and profit is achieved.

In this section of the Workbook we will be looking at how you, as a manager, can face up to these demands for an ethical approach in business, and the ways in which you can contribute to building awareness of ethical issues throughout your organization.

What's all the fuss about ethics?

In recent years the UK has been rocked by business scandals. Guinness, Maxwell, Polly Peck, BCCI and Barings Bank have all become linked, in the nation's mind, with unethical business behaviour. As we move towards the millennium, more and more businesses are beginning to realize that ethical behaviour is likely to be one of the keys to their future success and stability. Increasingly, in the minds of both shareholders and consumers, ethics are considered to be equally as important as profit. Both investors and consumers want to be connected with businesses which are seen to be operating ethically, within the law and with a measure of care and concern for the environment.

For any organization, the first steps towards achieving a culture which incorporates ethical behaviour and values into its day-to-day activities are setting out a code of ethics, and then making sure that everyone in the business understands and applies the code.

What is ethical behaviour?

Here are some of the responses given by senior managers working in profit-driven organizations when they were asked to give a definition of 'ethical behaviour':

- Knowing what's right and doing what's right
- Behaving honestly, openly and with fairness towards customers and employees
- Not only staying within the law but also always acting with honour and integrity
- Behaving in a way that lets me go to sleep at night with a clear conscience
- Knowing that everything we do could be reported, in detail, in the papers tomorrow – and we wouldn't need to worry.

What is unethical behaviour?

Unethical behaviour can be demonstrated by both individual employees and the organization as a whole.

ACTIVITY 1

In the space below, list six examples of the kind of behaviour which you would describe as unethical.

1

2

3

4

5

6

FEEDBACK

In every organization there are numerous opportunities for unethical behaviour.

- *Business conduct*
  - tax evasion
  - insider share dealing
  - inaccurate accounting
  - giving gifts or financial rewards in an attempt to influence business decisions
  - giving/receiving extravagant gifts or hospitality
  - lengthy delay in settling suppliers' debts
  - overcharging clients
  - being dishonest with customers
  - providing shoddy goods or services
  - excessive salaries for senior managers
- *Company relationships with employees*
  - providing unsafe working conditions
  - allowing/ignoring discrimination and/or harassment
  - insensitive handling of redundancies and/or disciplinary and grievance procedures
  - linking salary too closely to commission
  - pegging pay to the lowest possible levels
  - giving rewards for reasons other than work-related performance
- *Employee relationships with employers and colleagues*
  - stealing other people's ideas and claiming them as your own
  - stealing company time through unnecessary absence and lateness
  - stealing company money through personal faxes, e-mail and phone calls; overtime that hasn't been worked or expenses which haven't actually been paid out
  - stealing company property such as pens, paper, files, etc.
  - drug and/or alcohol abuse at work
- *External relationships*
  - paying bribes, making promises or falsifying information in order to win contracts
  - causing environmental damage
  - wasting natural resources
  - making large financial donations to political parties
  - creating business/financial links with oppressive regimes
- *Information*
  - ignoring confidential status of information
  - spreading misleading information about competitors
  - condoning misrepresentation in advertising or PR campaigns
  - withholding important information from shareholders and other important stakeholders

Ethical choices

When making decisions, everyone has the option to choose between 'doing the right thing' (the ethical choice) and doing 'the most desirable thing' (in many situations this is often the unethical choice). Where do you and your organization stand on ethics?

Consider the following statements and then tick the appropriate box depending on whether you strongly agree, agree, disagree or strongly disagree.

	Strongly agree	Agree	Disagree	Strongly disagree
My organization is very clear about the standards of conduct which I am expected to follow				
My organization expects me to keep within the law, but there is little discussion about ethical behaviour				
My organization expects me to put profits first, way in front of ethics				
In my organization, the most senior managers provide a clear lead for everyone else with regard to ethical behaviour				
In my organization we pay lip-service to ethical behaviour, but the reality is quite different				
I always comply with my organization's standards of conduct and professional code of ethics				
I make a determined effort to consistently do the right thing, rather than the easy thing				
I feel that, in my organization, I could speak out about ethical matters and be heard				
I use my own discretion when faced with ethical dilemmas at work				
I am more concerned about getting the job done than I am about complex ethical issues				
I believe that, as a manager, it is very important for me to give clear leadership on ethical values				
If I was faced with an ethical dilemma which could be damaging to my organization, I would do what I could to cover up the problem				

FEEDBACK

Research[2] shows that there is a strong link between ethical expectations in an organization and an individual's willingness to be active on ethical issues. In practice, what this means is that if ethics are high on the company's agenda, then the managers there will actively seek to demonstrate and encourage ethical values and behaviours. In organizations where limited importance is placed on ethics, managers are less likely to speak out about such matters.

Philip, a Customer Service Manager, explains:

Since I joined my present company I've had a lot of difficulty squaring my own conscience with some of our company practices and procedures. There have been two or three occasions when I've felt very strongly that, as an organization, we were not behaving ethically – but I have a large mortgage and a growing family. Until I can move on, I just swim with the tide and say nothing. Ethical behaviour is not something I discuss, either with colleagues or front-line staff – it's not part of the culture here.

Ted Johns[3] suggests that the factors which are most likely to influence people when they are choosing between taking the right action and the most desirable action are uncertainty, insecurity, ambition, laziness or the desire to have 'street cred'.

SHALL I DO THE 'RIGHT THING', OR THE 'EASY THING'?

Uncertainty

If people don't really know or understand their organization's policy, they will be unsure about what the company considers to be the 'right thing' to do. When people are unsure about what is expected of them, they will often opt for the easy route, and not think too much about the consequences of their actions.

Insecurity

When employees feel insecure or threatened at work they naturally focus more on their own needs than the needs of the organization. They will often respond with: 'They don't care about what happens to me, so why should I care about them?' As a result, people will take the 'easy' course of action, or behave in unethical ways, because they feel they have nothing to lose.

Ambition

People who are driven by ambition and who are desperate to succeed in their career can feel that 'the end justifies the means' and 'I'll do whatever it takes to get where I want to be'.

Laziness

People sometimes take short cuts and the easy route because doing the 'right thing' will involve a lot more time and effort.

'Street Cred'

In some companies, the senior people in the organization lead from the front, and operate on the basis that profit is the name of the game and ethical considerations are for wimps. In these businesses it is hardly surprising that others within the organization follow the example which has been set, and behave in a similar fashion.

ACTIVITY 3

Every manager in an organization can contribute towards influencing, to some extent, the culture of the business. Think about what you could do, as an individual, to demonstrate that you are behaving ethically, and want to encourage this kind of behaviour throughout the organization. List three things you could do:

1

2

3

Even though every organization is different, here are some guidelines as to how you can demonstrate your personal commitment to ethical behaviour.

- **Act honestly.** This involves being open, honest and above-board in all your dealings with people. This includes the people within the business, and external customers, contacts and suppliers. It means not having hidden agendas or secrets, not making promises you can't or won't keep, and not 'bending the truth' to gain a financial advantage. It also means using 'true scales, true weights, true measures' and giving value for money.
- **Act Fairly.** Fairness involves treating others equally and with equal care and consideration. Fair managers give equal weight to everyone's views and opinions and maintain equality when rewarding good performance. They don't bend the rules for a favoured few, or 'take against' people for personal reasons. Fair managers take their authority seriously, and exercise it fairly and without discrimination.
- **Act responsibly.** Managers, to one degree or another, have stewardship of people, resources and finance. Acting responsibly involves caring for those

people and things with integrity, and with due regard for their well-being.

- **Act respectfully.** Managers who act respectfully carefully consider and take into account the moral and legal rights of other people. They behave towards others in the same way that they would like to be treated themselves.

Bear in mind that everything you do and say sets an example. In just about every organization it is the managers who, by their behaviour and attitude, set the corporate culture. If the managers are seen to be economical with the truth, to 'wheel and deal' to get business, to cut corners, to ride roughshod over colleagues and play fast and loose with their expenses, then other staff will follow suit. If managers lead from the front with a dazzling display of unethical behaviour, then everyone in the business will assume that 'that's the way we do things around here'.

Ethical behaviour must be clearly and consistently demonstrated by managers before it can filter down to the rest of the employees. It has to be a case of 'Follow my lead, and do what I do', and not simply 'Don't watch me, just do as I say'.

Facing up to ethical dilemmas

Everyone, from time to time, has to face up to ethical dilemmas and make hard decisions. The next activity will give you an opportunity to consider some ethical dilemmas and think about how you might respond.

ACTIVITY 4

Read through the following case studies and note down, in the space provided, what you might do under similar circumstances.

CASE STUDY 1

Mike works as the Finance Director for a multinational pharmaceutical company based in the UK. All payments to suppliers must be authorized by him. Mike notices that the company has started to order chemicals from a new supplier at a significantly lower price. Surprised at the cost savings, Mike investigates. He discovers that the compounds involved are manufactured in Eastern Europe and shipped to the UK via Switzerland. He talks to various people in the company (research, quality control, export/import), and is told that compounds bought and shipped in this way are quite likely to be of inferior quality. If this were the case, then the compounds would affect the efficiency of the products manufactured and sold by his organization. Mike signals his concern to the Vice-President and is told 'There's nothing wrong with the compounds and the deal was too good to pass up. I'm not prepared to discuss this any further — just authorize payment.'

If you were in Mike's situation, what would you do?

CASE STUDY 2

Denise is the Training Manager for a chain of retail stores. Part of her remit is to employ external consultants to deliver training courses to staff based in stores around the country. Denise recruits the consultants, agrees the terms and conditions of their freelance contracts and generally oversees the work they do. She feels that it is extremely important for her organization to build and maintain good relationships with these external suppliers.

Over a period of nine months she receives numerous complaints from the external consultants that their invoices are not being paid on time. In some cases people are being made to wait up to six months before their invoices are paid, and for some of the consultants this is causing severe cash-flow problems. Denise discusses the situation with the Finance Manager and is told that: 'They'll just have to wait. We've got cash-flow problems ourselves and I'm more keen to pay other, more important suppliers. I'm sorry, there's nothing I can do about the situation for the time being.'

If you were in Denise's situation, what would you do?

CASE STUDY 3

Leo works as a Marketing Manager for a manufacturing company which produces a slimming food which is in direct competition with the market brand leader. Leo is called to a board meeting and informed that the company is going to launch a new slimming product which will 'sweep the country and take the major market share overnight'. Leo is asked to work with the company's advertising agency to create a new campaign.

Three months before the product launch Leo receives previously unpublished research data which clearly shows that the new product is totally useless and will not, under any circumstances, cause weight loss. He presents this information to the Marketing Director and is told: 'Well, it's too late now. We've invested too much to turn back – we'll have to run with it.'

If you were in Leo's situation, what would you do?

CASE STUDY 4

Marianne is hoping to be offered a partnership in the legal firm where she has practised for the past five years. The Senior Partner, without consultation, appoints his nephew as Practice Manager. During the course of conversation Marianne happens to mention this new appointment to a colleague from another law firm. She is informed that the new Practice Manager was fired from his previous job because of complaints of sexual harassment made by female staff members. He subsequently presented his case to an Industrial Tribunal and lost. Marianne's colleague said: 'To be honest, we wouldn't touch him with a bargepole. Not only did he upset some of the staff he was working with, but there were complaints from female clients as well.'

If you were in Marianne's situation, what would you do?

FEEDBACK

Decision making can be tough. To quote from the Institute of Management's Code of Conduct:

It is usual for professional managers to encounter circumstances or situations in which various values, principles, rules and interests appear to conflict, and may be difficult to harmonise in practice. No ready answer can be given for all such conflicts.

In each of the situations described above, the easy thing to do (and probably the safest, from a job security point of view) would be to say nothing, 'put your head down' and ignore the problem. Here are some alternatives:

CASE STUDY 1

■ Mike could ask people in Quality Control to run exhaustive tests on the compounds in an attempt to come up with some hard data. If the results confirmed his worst fears, he could then present the evidence to the Vice-President. If this action didn't produce the response he hoped for, Mike could then send the data to Head Office in the US. He would, of course, have to recognize that Head Office may already be aware of the situation and his data would be 'old news'

- Mike could refuse to authorize payment for the compounds, and then wait to see how the Vice-President responded
- Mike could put his concerns in writing to the Vice-President and ask him to reconsider his position
- Mike could use the organization's formal mechanism (if there is one) to express his concern
- Mike could blow the whistle by leaking information to the media
- Mike could resign

CASE STUDY 2

- Denise could negotiate with the Finance Manager to offer the consultants a 25 per cent up-front payment (paid before the work is carried out), with the remainder of the invoice to be paid 90 days after completion of the work
- Denise could use the organization's formal mechanism (if there is one) to express her concern
- Denise could put her concerns in writing to the Finance Manager, and copy the document to the Managing Director or Chairman of the Board
- Denise could refuse to issue further freelance contracts to consultants until she is able to negotiate a better deal for them

CASE STUDY 3

- Leo, working closely with the advertising agency, could do his best to ensure that the marketing campaign is appropriate for the product
- Leo could negotiate for additional funding to run a different study on the efficiency of the product, in the hope that the data will be more favourable second time around
- Leo could use the organization's formal mechanism (if there is one) to express his concern
- Leo could send the unpublished research data to the Managing Director or Chairman of the Board
- Leo could refuse to work on the project
- Leo could resign

CASE STUDY 4

- Marianne could have a quiet word with the new Practice Manager to alert him to the fact that she is aware of his history
- Marianne could make it her business to monitor the new Practice Manager for the first six months of his appointment

- Marianne could discuss her concerns with the Senior Partner
- Marianne could arrange for a senior colleague within the firm to mention the matter to the Senior Partner
- Marianne could use the organization's formal mechanism (if there is one) to express her concern
- Marianne could arrange for the person who originally alerted her to the situation to mention the matter to the Senior Partner

Many people, faced with similar dilemmas, find themselves speaking out publicly and being labelled as whistle-blowers. Sadly, research has shown that a study of 233 whistle-blowers revealed that 84 per cent of these people were fired as a result of their actions.[4] Government opposition to the Public Interest Disclosure Bill means that whistle-blowers do not yet have a great deal of protection but, hopefully in the future, this will change.

Texas Instruments have devised a seven-step plan for their employees to use to help them determine whether or not a decision or course of action is ethical.

REACHING AN ETHICAL DECISION

When faced with an ethical dilemma which requires a decision, ask yourself the following questions, based on the Texas Instruments seven-step test[5]:

1 Is what I want to do legal? **If it isn't legal, then stop now, don't do it.**
2 Does what I want to do comply with the company's values? **If it doesn't fit, then stop here – don't do it.**
3 If I do what I want to do, how will I feel about it? Will I be able to live with it? Will my conscience be clear? **If your conscience isn't likely to be clear, then stop. Don't do it.**
4 If I do what I want to do, and it hits the newspaper headlines tomorrow, how would I feel? If my decision or action was broadcast to the nation in the morning, would I regret doing what I had done? **If so, stop. Don't do it.**
5 If I do what I want to do, what could go wrong? What would be the effects for the business and for me, personally? **If there are likely to be serious negative consequences, stop. Don't do it.**
6 Do I know, deep down, that what I want to do is wrong? **If so, stop now, don't do it.**
7 Am I unsure about whether or not what I want to do is wrong? **If so, stop and ask someone else in the business. Keep on asking until you get an answer.**

Think back to a time when, as a manager, you were faced with an ethical dilemma. Consider the following questions and note down your answers in the spaces provided.

1   What, precisely, was the ethical dilemma?

2   How did you resolve the dilemma? What decision did you reach?

3   What was the outcome of your decision? Were there any repercussions?

4   Do you believe you did the right thing? Or do you regret the decision? If so, why?

5   If, when reaching your decision, you had addressed the seven questions outlined on page 13, would you have reached a different decision?

6   Would the outcome have been different? If so, in what way?

Clearly, the situation you faced and the decision you reached will be personal to you. You may have responded to this activity by coming to the conclusion that, if you were faced with the same situation again, you would behave in exactly the same way. On the other hand, looking back, you may feel that if you had used the seven-step test or had the benefit of a code of ethics, then the outcome would have been very different.

Creating a code of ethical conduct

A *code of ethics* is a set of guidelines based on moral principles or values. Organizations create and use their code of ethical conduct in order to provide a clear framework for acceptable, ethical behaviour. The guidelines should be used to influence the conduct of both employees and the organization as a whole, and should be applied to all business activities undertaken. This means both internal activities, carried out within the company, and external activities, undertaken outside the company.

ADVANTAGES OF A CODE OF ETHICAL CONDUCT

For managers and employees

- Everyone in the business knows precisely what is expected of them, and what the organization considers to be ethical and unethical behaviour. There are no 'grey areas'

For the organization

- It sends a clear signal to suppliers, competitors and customers that the organization is serious about and committed to ethical standards

For shareholders

- It inspires public confidence and enhances the organization's reputation

DISADVANTAGES OF A CODE OF ETHICAL CONDUCT

- The code must be a genuine working document, and not just a paper exercise. Making it work can take up a considerable amount of senior management time
- Everyone in the organization must interpret and be guided by the code in the same way. If people in Harrogate perceive the code in a different way to the people in London, then the document ultimately becomes worthless

A good example of a straightforward document is the *Institute of Management's Code of Conduct and Guides to Professional Management Practice.*

Institute of Management Code of Conduct

At all times a member shall uphold the good standing and reputation of the profession of management; and while practising as a manager shall:

- Have due regard for and comply with relevant law
- Not misuse or abuse power or position
- Follow the Guides to Professional Management Practice, as approved by the Council
- Have a duty to provide information on request to any committee or sub-committee of the Institute established to investigate any alleged breach of this Code

This document is offered as guidance to members in the discharge of their professional responsibilities. It sets out principles, approaches and guidelines which can be applied in different contexts by an individual's judgement. A Code and Guides such as these cannot claim to be comprehensive, so where dilemmas remain, appropriate discussion of the issues requiring resolution is seen as a professional duty.

1   A professional man or woman is one who justifiably claims to provide an expert service of value to society, and who accepts the duties entailed by that claim; including:

- the attainment and maintenance of high standards of education, training and practical judgement, and
- honouring the special trust reposed by clients, employers, colleagues, and the general public

2   The professional discharge of such duties within management entails:

- the application of expert knowledge and judgement in the field of operations, and
- the motivation and control of the activities of others, and
- a contribution to the joint achievement of objectives of the organization, so far as this is possible and proper

3   The discharge of one's duties as a professional manager also involves the acceptance and habitual exercise of ethical values, among which a high place should be accorded to integrity, honesty, loyalty and fairness

4   It is usual for professional managers to encounter circumstances or situations in which various values, principles, rules and interests appear to conflict, and may be difficult to harmonise in practice. No ready answer can be given for all such conflicts. The best resources which can be brought to bear are the professional and personal characteristics and qualities already identified

5   Nevertheless, there are certain recurring situations which could give rise to concern, in which the best professional judgement and practice should normally be considered to be as described in the Guides to Professional Management Practice

The Code of Conduct forms part of a Byelaw made under Articles 10, 11 and 12 of the Articles of Association of The Institute of Management. It prescribes the standards which any Committee established by the Council for the purpose may take into account in considering the conduct of a member of the Institute; but so that the Committee shall not be prevented from taking other matters into consideration. Any member contravening any section of the Code may be liable to disciplinary action which could result in expulsion from the Institute.

Guides to Professional Management Practice

1. As regards the Individual Manager
The Professional Manager should:

- Comply with any contract of employment or other agreement existing between an employer and the manager, allowing due reservation for matters of conscience
- Identify and attempt to resolve conflicts of values, including ethical values, using a carefully reasoned approach
- Pursue integrity and competence in all managerial activity
- Take active steps for continuing development of personal competence
- Take responsibility for safeguarding the security of confidential information
- Exhaust all available internal remedies for dealing with matters perceived as improper, before considering any other action
- Openly declare any personal interest which might be seen to influence managerial decisions

2. As regards others within the organization
The Professional Manager should, in addition to the above:

- Take full account of the needs, pressures and problems of others, and not discriminate on grounds other than those demonstrably necessary to the task
- Seek to avoid asking others to do something which offends their conscience
- Fully consider the mental and physical health, safety and well-being of others

- Encourage and assist others to develop their potential
- Be concerned with the development of quality in all management matters, including quality of life
- Ensure that all are aware of their responsibilities, areas of authority and accountability, and methods of their review and reward for contribution

3. As regards the organization

The Professional Manager should, in addition to the above:

- Agree and uphold lawful policies and practices within the organization
- Ensure the identification and communication of relevant policies, practices and information
- Review organization structure and procedures as to their suitability for achieving objectives
- Disseminate information on factors likely to require change in the organization
- Seek to balance departmental aims in furtherance of the organization's overall objectives

4. As regards others external to but in direct relationship with the organization

The Professional Manager should, in addition to the above:

- Ensure that the interests of others are properly identified and responded to in a balanced manner
- Establish and develop a continuing and satisfactory relationship based on mutual confidence
- Avoid entering into arrangements which unlawfully or improperly affect competitive practice
- Neither offer nor accept any gift, favour or hospitality intended as, or having the effect of, bribery and corruption
- In the public interest, co-operate with others to uphold the law and to arrive at the truth in investigations and disciplinary processes

5. As regards UK society and environment

The Professional Manager should, in addition to the above:

- Have due regard to the short- and long-term effects and possible consequences within society of present and proposed actions
- Be willing to contribute to and comment upon the manageability of proposed legislation and the running of social affairs
- Communicate to the public truthfully and without intent to mislead by slanting or suppressing information
- Seek to conserve resources wherever possible, especially those which are non-renewable
- Seek to avoid destruction of resources by pollution and have a contingency plan for limiting destruction in the event of a disaster

6. As regards overseas societies and environments

The Professional Manager should, in addition to the above:

- Be aware of the management implications of global environmental issues
- Decline to solve UK problems of pollution and processes by their export unchanged to the detriment of the quality of life of other societies
- Have due regard to the possibility that satisfactory practice in the UK might be offensive or misleading elsewhere
- Respect the customs, practices and reasonable ambitions of other peoples
- Wherever practicable, comply with the professional standards set out in the Code of Conduct and these Guides, but not necessarily deemed to be in breach of obligations as a member of the Institute if complying with established overseas customs and practices which are inconsistent in detail with the foregoing.

Spreading the word about ethical behaviour

Sometimes an organization has to face up to unethical management practices under the spotlight of 'bad press'. This happened with Hoover, when the company was overtaken by the negative publicity surrounding the free flight tickets promotion. Union Carbine suffered a similar fate because of the poisonous gas leak in Bhopal, India.

When share prices fall or sales figures take a nose-dive, it is the shareholders or consumers who push companies into re-evaluating their approach to ethical practices. Sometimes it is the top tier of management who recognize that their competitive advantage lies in demonstrating that the organization is committed, in a big way, to ethical values. One example of this is The Body Shop, who heavily publicize their commitment to 'green' and environmentally friendly products.

Whatever the reasons for highlighting the need to re-evaluate ethical concerns within a company, it is always necessary to spread the word top-down, from managers to employees.

ACTIVITY 6   C6.3

There are a number of key actions which any organization can take to communicate to staff that the company is serious about ethical practices and behaviour. List, in the space below, four key actions your company could take to encourage employees to take an ethical approach at work.

1

2

3

4

FEEDBACK There are eleven key steps which any organization can take to encourage ethical behaviour at work.

KEY STEP 1 LEAD FROM THE FRONT BY EXAMPLE

Any organization which is serious about ethics must make sure that the managers drive the programme through. The commitment of the top tier of management must be genuine, and should be seen and felt throughout the company. Where possible, a very senior, high-profile person within the organization should be appointed to lead the way and be seen as the manager with ultimate responsibility for making the change happen. Needless to say, this person should be committed, heart and mind, to creating an environment where ethical practices lie at the core of the business.

KEY STEP 2 EXPLAIN TO STAFF *WHY* ETHICS ARE IMPORTANT AND *HOW* THEY CAN DEMONSTRATE ETHICAL BEHAVIOUR

Staff should be able to understand the benefits and advantages of ethical behaviour. For example, two important benefits are:

- If everything we do and say is ethical, then no-one inside or outside the company can point a finger at the way we do business ... so we won't make headlines in the tabloid press.
- Customers are, more than ever before, environmentally aware. Companies which become involved in practices which damage the environment will lose business. Loss of business ultimately has a knock-on effect on profits and job security.

If staff are unclear about what is and what is not ethical, then doubts, anxieties and cynicism can creep in, so explanations are very important.

KEY STEP 3 CREATE A DRAFT CODE

Consult all available documentation. This may include legal guidelines, policy documents and standard Codes such as those published by the Institute of Business Ethics and the Institute of Management.

Rather than imposing a 'shopping list' of ethical values and behaviours, involve employees in the process. Give staff the opportunity to consider how everyone in the company can work together to create an organization which is based on ethical values. Once employees take **ownership** of the concept of ethical behaviour, they will want to make it work. Ownership grows out of involvement, and provides a real sense of pride and commitment:

- 'That was my idea ...'
- 'I suggested that ...'
- 'I stuck my neck out and said we should do that, so I'm going to make sure that it works.'

The draft code should include:

- An introduction which explains the purpose of the code and why it is important
- A statement defining the organization's mission and objectives
- Clear guidance on what constitutes proper, ethical behaviour when dealing with relationships and situations arising between:
    - organization and employee
    - employee and organization
    - employee and colleagues
    - organization/employees and customers, suppliers, shareholders, stakeholders and so on
- Straightforward guidelines on operating principles, together with real-life examples
- Details of a formal system which employees can use to resolve concerns, questions and difficult or unusual situations. This mechanism is important because, if an organization has clear communication channels, staff can use these to highlight unethical practices and there

will be no need for public whistle-blowing

- Keep it simple. The code should provide clear, easy-to-understand advice and guidelines which allow people to quickly grasp, without jargon or techno-speak, what is and what is not acceptable
- Be realistic. The code should be a practical, working document. If there is an enormous gap between the code and working practices, then the code will fall by the wayside
- Check that the code agrees with information and guidelines given in staff handbooks and operating manuals. (You may find that you need to change either the code or the handbooks and manuals.)

KEY STEP 4 CIRCULATE THE CODE AND INVITE FEEDBACK

Ask for feedback from everyone within the organization. This will help to advertise and market the code, and will also show employees that you are serious about encouraging their involvement and commitment. Constructive criticism should be encouraged so that adjustments can be made where necessary. Employees should be able to voice their opinions and concerns without fear of falling out of favour or being out of a job.

Take feedback seriously, and don't just view the consultation process as a paper exercise. Where major revisions are made to the code, circulate the revised draft so that everyone can see that comments have been acknowledged.

KEY STEP 5 DEVISE AN IMPLEMENTATION STRATEGY AND PUT IT INTO PRACTICE

Once the code is finalized, if the organization is serious, then it must be applied in a practical way. Let people know that this is a continuous programme, not just a flavour-of-the-month big new idea which will quietly disappear over time. Incorporate the code into induction, staff training and management development programmes. Practical training sessions in which employees address specific ethical dilemmas will provide clear-cut guidelines on acceptable behaviour, and will also help to make ethics at work real and relevant.

KEY STEP 6 DISTRIBUTE THE FINAL DRAFT CODE THROUGHOUT THE ORGANIZATION

Everyone in the business, without exception, should receive a copy of the code. The document should be accompanied by a letter from the most senior person in the organization, explaining the purpose of the code and detailing expectations about its use.

KEY STEP 7 IMPLEMENT A FORMAL SYSTEM FOR TROUBLE-SHOOTING

The mechanism for resolving questions and problems should be operational from the day employees receive their copy of the code document. The system could be set up so as to involve the employee's line manager, human resource department or a dedicated 'ethics hotline'. Whatever system you choose, do make sure that it is up and running, otherwise people will quickly become disillusioned if they can't get the answers they need when they need them.

Be aware that employees may need help and guidance with:

1 Trouble-shooting in connection with ethical matters external to the organization ('I am concerned about a supplier (or a customer, or a competitor) ...')
2 Whistle-blowing in connection with ethical matters inside the organization ('I am concerned about what is happening in the Research Department ...')

In the case of whistle-blowing within the organization, it should be made crystal clear to employees that **malicious and unfounded** allegations of wrongdoing, such as fraud, malpractice, mismanagement, breaches of health & safety regulations and so on, will result in disciplinary action against the whistle-blower.

It is important, however, to protect whistle-blowers who are acting with honest and sincere intentions. These people need to know that they will have the support of the organization, and that there will be no reprisals or discrimination against them. Some companies allow employees to voice their concerns anonymously (although once an investigation gets under way, in almost all cases their identity, one way or another, is revealed).

To help avoid instances of whistle-blowing to the media, remind staff that:

- approaches for confidential advice to outside parties, such as trade unions or lawyers, are acceptable
- disclosure of confidential information is prohibited by their contract of employment (the duty of fidelity is implied by the law in every contract of employment).

KEY STEP 8 ESTABLISH A FAIR AND IMPARTIAL INVESTIGATIVE PROCEDURE

Once a member of staff has identified a concern, it is the organization's responsibility to follow it through and discover the truth of the matter. Failure to do this will signal to employees that the organization is not seriously committed to the programme.

A swift response will reassure the person making the allegations, will to some extent reduce stress and speculation, and should, hopefully, reduce the risk of retaliation or harassment by the 'accused'.

KEY STEP 9 ESTABLISH A MECHANISM TO MONITOR PROGRESS

It is important to review the code's continuing relevance and to monitor impact, reaction and feedback. Nine months to a year after the code's introduction would be a good time to analyse progress. This could be done through a review of the 'ethics hotline' results and, perhaps, by further consultation with employees on a group and one-to-one basis.

KEY STEP 10 REWARD ETHICAL BEHAVIOUR

If ethical behaviour is reinforced by a reward system, and unethical behaviour is punished, then employees will quickly see that the organization is serious. Although it may seem inappropriate to have to use a 'carrot and stick' approach to get people to do what is right, offering incentives and penalties does produce positive results.

KEY STEP 11 BE PATIENT!

Change doesn't happen overnight. Be prepared for slow but steady progress, and recognize that, from time to time, there will be disappointments and set-backs.

Your personal contribution

The important question which individual managers need to address is: 'What can I do, at a personal level, to encourage and support ethical behaviour in the business?'

ACTIVITY 7

Begin by thinking about the kinds of unethical behaviour which are most likely to crop up in your organization. List these in the left-hand column. Then, for each example you have identified, think about the practical things you can personally do, as a manager, to encourage ethical behaviour and choices within your organization. List these in the right-hand column.

Unethical behaviour	Positive action I can take

FEEDBACK

Examples of unethical behaviour which are most likely to occur in your company will, to some extent, depend on the culture and values of the organization. Your solutions will therefore be fairly specific to the business in which you are involved, but here are some suggestions which can be utilized by everyone:

■ Make sure that you personally thoroughly understand and comply with the legislation, industry regulations, professional and organizational codes of ethics which affect the work you do and the organization which employs you

■ Go out of your way to ensure that other people have the necessary information about legislation, regulations and codes of ethics. If necessary, organize additional training so that everyone is clear about what is expected of them.

■ Be very clear, in your own mind, about what is and what is not ethical behaviour

■ Consider the implications of everything you do, and ask yourself:
  – How will this affect the employees?
  – How will this impact on the shareholders and other important stakeholders?
  – Is this the right thing to do, or is it the easy option?

■ Deal with people fairly, honestly and respectfully

■ Set a good example

■ Recognize that ethical dilemmas are often not clear-cut choices between 'right' and 'wrong'. Business decisions often involve numerous people and large amounts of money. Making the decision which is ethical and in line with corporate policy often requires careful, cautious and reasoned thought

Summary

■ Ethical behaviour is about understanding the difference between the 'desirable action' and the 'right action', and then taking the 'right action'

■ Ethical (and unethical) behaviour can be demonstrated in the key areas of:
  ■ business conduct
  ■ company relationships with employees
  ■ employee relationships with employers and colleagues
  ■ external relationships
  ■ information

■ When considering whether or not what you want to do is ethical, ask yourself:
  ■ Is it legal?
  ■ Does it comply with the company's values?
  ■ If I do it, will my conscience be clear?
  ■ If what I want to do made headlines tomorrow, how would I feel?
  ■ What could go wrong? And how would I feel about it?

- Do I know, deep down, that this is wrong?
- Am I unsure about whether or not this is wrong?

The answers to these questions will help you to recognize whether or not your proposed action is ethical.

- The eleven key steps your organization can take in order to encourage and gain commitment to ethical behaviour are:
  - lead from the front by example
  - explain to staff why ethics are important and how they can demonstrate ethical behaviour
  - create a draft code of ethics
  - circulate the code and invite feedback
  - devise an implementation strategy and put it into practice
  - distribute the final code throughout the organization
  - implement a formal system for trouble-shooting
  - establish a fair and impartial investigative procedure
  - establish a mechanism to monitor progress
  - reward ethical behaviour
  - be patient!

Notes

1 Brigley, Stephen (1994) *Walking the Tightrope; a survey of ethics in management*, Institute of Management.

2 Brigley, Stephen (1994) *Walking the Tightrope; a survey of ethics in management*, Institute of Management.

3 Johns, Ted (1995) 'Don't be afraid of the moral maze', *People Management*, 5 October, vo.l 1, no. 20, pp. 32–34.

4 Johns, Ted (1995) 'Don't be afraid of the moral maze', *People Management*, 5 October, vol. 1, no. 20, pp 32–34.

5 Flynn, Gillian (1995) 'Make employees ethics your business', *Personnel Journal*, June, pp 30–32, 34, 36, 38–39, 41.

Section 2 Planning and prioritizing objectives

Introduction

Objectives (which some people refer to as goals, aims, outcomes or targets) give direction and purpose to our lives. They help us to become clear about what we want to achieve, at work and in our personal lives. Once we know **where** we are going, we can then start to think about **how** we are going to get there.

In this section we are going to be looking at the process of setting achievable objectives, and then we are going to examine how you can prioritize those objectives so that you deal with your issues in a sensible order. If the key step of prioritizing is skipped over in a superficial way, or missed out altogether, then you can find yourself wasting time doing the wrong things, or doing the right things in the wrong order.

In this Workbook we are focusing on team, group and corporate objectives. In Workbook 2, *Managing Yourself*, we will be looking at techniques that you can use to set personal work objectives which will enable you to manage your time more efficiently and effectively, and in Workbook 12, *Developing Yourself and Your Staff*, we will be looking at the process of setting those personal life objectives which relate to long-term career developments.

Where are you going?

Objectives are like road maps. They help us to:

- define where we want to go
- plan the most appropriate route
- check to see how close we are to our final destination
- confirm that we have arrived

You may use either *objective*, *aim*, *target*, *goal* or *outcome* to describe a statement which summarizes what an organization, a team or an individual is hoping to achieve. These words are all interchangeable, and mean the same thing. For the sake of simplicity, we are using the word *objective* throughout this Workbook.

ACTIVITY 8

Think back to work situations in which you have been involved where planning and prioritizing objectives has been largely ignored or mismanaged at the outset of the project. What were the effects on:

(a) the project?
(b) the team?
(c) individual members of the team?

(a) Effect on the project

Not planning and prioritizing objectives before the work started had the following effects on the project:

1

2

3

(b) Effect on the team

Not planning and prioritizing objectives before the work started had the following effects on the team:

1

2

3

(c) Effect on the individual team members

Not planning and prioritizing objectives before the work started had the following effects on the individual team members:

1

2

3

The effects of not planning and prioritizing clear and specific objectives mean that managers can take time-consuming detours and often find themselves a long way away from where they want to be. This can have disastrous results for the project, and everyone involved.

EFFECTS ON THE PROJECT

- Time schedules and budgets become meaningless. Because there are no clear objectives, people are unaware of the time-frame and the resources available. Consequently, work is late and costs escalate. When things begin to go wrong, ill-considered objectives are set as a response to an emergency situation. Pressure begins to mount and, as unexpected (and inevitable) problems and delays occur, the time schedules and budgets become a movable feast. Instead of working to clear deadlines, dates and amounts are set **in the hope that they can be reached**. If the new objectives are not met, then they are moved again.

- Quality standards become meaningless. Because of external pressure about time and money, panic sets in and people start to cut corners just to get the job finished. Sometimes this means that inferior resources are used because of the delays involved in acquiring what is best. Sometimes this means that people make rash decisions or produce inferior designs or resort to recycling old, worn-out ideas. There simply isn't time to produce their best work.

EFFECTS ON THE TEAM

- People are unsure of what is expected of them. They 'think' they know; they 'hope' they know. In new or insecure teams, people will hesitate before asking too many questions because they do not want to be perceived as 'the one person who doesn't understand'. Consequently, team members can find themselves working towards different objectives, which will, of course, produce very different end results.

- As confusion grows, time schedules are overshot and spending goes over budget allocations. The pressure on the team steadily increases. Interest, motivation and commitment decrease as people begin to wish that the project was finished and out of the way.

- Co-operation and communication between team members begins to break down. People become defensive and start to blame each other for delays and problems. In many cases, cliques form. Quite often, the project manager is held solely responsible for everything that has gone wrong.

EFFECTS ON THE INDIVIDUAL

- As the project spirals down into a disaster zone, individuals lose confidence and self-esteem. Decision making becomes ever more difficult, and no-one wants to use their initiative in case they make things even worse.

■ People begin to feel extremely stressed, and ill-health and absenteeism become a fact of life. As more people take time off work, the project slides deeper into disarray.

Setting SMART objectives

The key to success is to set *SMART* objectives at the outset. The keyword SMART will help you to remember that objectives should be:

> **S**imple
> **M**easurable
> **A**chievable
> **R**ealistic
> **T**ime-related

SIMPLE OBJECTIVES

An objective should be a statement which defines the end result you want to achieve. It should be *simple*, clear and easy to understand. Unclear, complex or convoluted objectives may look very grand on paper, but are not so easy to understand six months later, when you are in the process of reviewing progress. Simple objectives allow everyone involved – team players, subordinates, managers – to quickly see what you plan to achieve. For example:

■ **Unclear, complex objectives** would be:
  1 Seek to disseminate information using technological advances in order to reach a previously untapped global market
  2 Challenge our competition in the marketplace in order to achieve a sustainable increase in our market share
  3 Relocate our operational base to a dynamic and forward-looking environment which will enable us to participate in faster growth opportunities
■ **Simple objectives** would be:
  1 Create a Home Page and web site on the World Wide Web
  2 Increase our market share
  3 Move our existing offices to Reading

MEASURABLE OBJECTIVES

Objectives should be *measurable*. They should allow you to measure progress and achievement. You need to know where you are going, what you hope to achieve, and whether or not you are meeting the standards you have set.

- **Simple, measurable objectives** would be:
  1 Create a **5-megabyte** Home Page and web site on the World Wide Web
  2 Increase our market share **in the UK by 26 per cent**
  3 Move **all staff** currently working in our existing offices to Reading

ACHIEVABLE OBJECTIVES

The key question to ask yourself when setting objectives, is: 'Is this *achievable*?' Setting objectives which are unlikely to be achieved is a pointless exercise. Anyone who is charged with meeting an unachievable objective will quickly become demoralized and demotivated. Simon, a Production Manager from Aberdeen, explains:

We'd taken delivery of a new piece of machinery which was far in advance of anything we'd handled before. The technology was very complex, and our people needed new skills and new ways of working. Our objective was to start production in the autumn, six months away. We ran Assessment Centres to create new teams and team leaders, and as soon as we'd completed the selection process we began the actual hands-on training. At that time, we were right on schedule. In the middle of all this activity the MD told me he'd changed things around and we had to be up and running in seven days' time. It couldn't be achieved and, to be honest, I think he knew it. I love a challenge, but this was Mission Impossible, and I told him so. It caused a lot of bad feeling with the teams. They felt that he just didn't understand what was involved. Naturally, we didn't achieve the new objective, and everyone felt disenchanted with the project and thoroughly demotivated.

REALISTIC OBJECTIVES

Once objectives have been clarified and set, they should not be altered without good reason. Sometimes, of course, external factors such as economic, legislative or competitive changes mean that objectives have to be revisited and rewritten. If this is necessary, do make sure that the new objective meets the criteria of *smart, measurable, achievable, realistic* and, of course, *time-related*.

TIME-RELATED OBJECTIVES

Because it is important to constantly monitor progress in relation to objectives, you need to include a *time-frame* within which the objective should be achieved. Doing this will allow you, week by week and month by month, to check to see whether you are on target for achievement, or whether adjustments need to be made.

- **Time-related objectives** would be:
  1 Create a 5-megabyte Home Page and web site on the World Wide Web by **15th December 1996**
  2 Increase our market share in the UK by 26 per cent **by 1 April 1997**
  3 Move all staff currently working in our existing offices to Reading **by 30 March 1997**

ACTIVITY 9

Think back to the most recent team project in which you were involved. Note down (1) your individual objectives and (2) the team's objectives. Assess these objectives against the criteria of Simple, Measurable, Achievable, Realistic, Time-related. Where necessary, rewrite the objectives to make them SMART.

Name of project:
Date of completion:

Tick whichever boxes apply

1 My individual objectives

Objective (a)	Simple	Yes ❑	No ❑
	Measurable	Yes ❑	No ❑
	Achievable	Yes ❑	No ❑
	Realistic	Yes ❑	No ❑
	Time-related	Yes ❑	No ❑

To match the SMART criteria, this objective could be rewritten as:

Objective (b)	Simple	Yes ❑	No ❑
	Measurable	Yes ❑	No ❑
	Achievable	Yes ❑	No ❑
	Realistic	Yes ❑	No ❑
	Time-related	Yes ❑	No ❑

To match the SMART criteria, this objective could be rewritten as:

2   The team's objectives:

Objective (a)   Simple   Yes ❑   No ❑

Measurable   Yes ❑   No ❑

Achievable   Yes ❑   No ❑

Realistic   Yes ❑   No ❑

Time-Related   Yes ❑   No ❑

To match the SMART criteria, this objective could be rewritten as:

Objective (b)   Simple   Yes ❑   No ❑

Measurable   Yes ❑   No ❑

Achievable   Yes ❑   No ❑

Realistic   Yes ❑   No ❑

Time-related   Yes ❑   No ❑

To match the SMART criteria, this objective could be rewritten as:

FEEDBACK

The key point here is to make sure that, once having created an objective, it meets the SMART criteria. Failure to do this can result in expensive delays, lost business and unsatisfactory teamwork.

Planning

For any manager wishing to achieve a specific outcome, the first step is to clarify and write down the objectives. This should done regardless of whether the outcome is related to a specific project:

■ By 30 August 1997, customer database to be updated to include everyone who has purchased since 1 January 1992

■ Carry out total stock inventory by 22 June 1997

or related to a broader, ongoing aspect of activity:

- Ensure that the weekly team meetings are attended by every team member who is on site that day
- Speed the flow of information through the department so that everyone has the relevant data by 10 a.m. each Monday morning

The next step is to break down each objective into a series of separate tasks.

ACTIVITY 10

For the purpose of this activity, assume that you have been given the following objective:

- By end of January 1997, and within existing budget, update our fleet of company cars, ensuring that all new vehicles are fitted with ABS and air-bags.

Your task is to:

1   List five pieces of information you would need before you could begin to break down the objective into separate tasks:

    1

    2

    3

    4

    5

2   List the separate tasks you would need to undertake in order to achieve your objective:

FEEDBACK

Before you could begin to plan how best to achieve your objective:

- By end of January 1997, and within existing budget, update our fleet of company cars, ensuring that all new vehicles are fitted with ABS and air-bags

You would need answers to the following questions:

- What is the existing budget? Is this an absolute, or is there any room for an increase?
- How many cars are in the existing fleet?
- Is it an absolute requirement to obtain the same number of new cars? Might fewer or more be required? (Will any existing staff be leaving the company? Will any additional staff be joining the company?)
- Apart from the requirement for ABS and air-bags, are there any other requirements or restrictions? (Petrol or diesel? Engine size? Colours? Manual or automatic? In-car telephones? Vehicle recovery services?)
- Should all the new cars have the same specification, or will senior staff require 'extras' (Sun roof? CD player? Electric windows? Power steering?)
- Why is the update required? (Health and Safety? Company image? Tax advantage?)
- What is the absolute limit of my responsibility? (Do I need to confer with anyone during the process, or am I ultimately responsible for making the final decision?)
- Has there been a project similar to this in the past? Who was responsible? What happened? (This is important information, as you can learn from history and avoid past pitfalls.)

Once you have the answers to these questions, you can begin to list the individual tasks. These include:

- Investigate suitable replacement vehicles
- Agree vehicle specification (accessories, colours, etc.)
- Identify local dealerships
- Organize handover of new vehicles to staff
- Ensure that all old/new documentation is in order
- Agree delivery date
- Negotiate a price for the new vehicles
- Negotiate a price for the trade-in vehicles
- Allocate new vehicles to staff
- Organize finance

Prioritizing tasks

Once you know what it is you have to achieve *(objective),* and you have identified the individual tasks involved *(e.g. investigate suitable replacement vehicles),* the next steps are to:

- *prioritize* the tasks
- *assign* a specific date for completion to each task

Prioritizing the tasks necessary to achieve the

- By end of January 1997, and within existing budget, update our fleet of company cars, ensuring that all new vehicles are fitted with ABS and air-bags

objective is fairly straightforward. Many of the tasks are obviously sequential and must be done in a specific order:

1 Agree vehicle specification (accessories, colours, etc.) by 12 September 1997
2 Identify local dealerships by 18 September 1997
3 Investigate suitable replacement vehicles by 18 October 1997
4 Negotiate a price for the new vehicles by 31 October 1997
5 Negotiate a price for the trade-in vehicles by 31 October 1997
6 Agree delivery date by 31 October 1997
7 Organize finance by 15 November 1997
8 Allocate new vehicles to staff by 10 December 1997
9 Ensure that all old/new documentation is in order by 26 January 1998
10 Organize handover of new vehicles to staff by 26 January 1998

In a flowchart, the process looks like this (Figure 1):

```
┌─────────────────────────┐
│ 1 Clarify the SMART      │
│ objective                │
└─────────────────────────┘
      ┌─────────────────────────┐
      │ 2 (a) Organize available │
      │ information (b) Obtain    │
      │ required information      │
      └─────────────────────────┘
            ┌─────────────────────────┐
            │ 3 Identify individual tasks │
            │ and assign a completion date │
            │ to each                   │
            └─────────────────────────┘
                  ┌─────────────────────────┐
                  │ 4 Prioritize tasks into a │
                  │ logical sequence          │
                  └─────────────────────────┘
                        ┌─────────────────────────┐
                        │ 5 Complete each task in   │
                        │ turn                      │
                        └─────────────────────────┘
                              ┌─────────────────────────┐
                              │ 6 Achieve the SMART       │
                              │ objective                 │
                              └─────────────────────────┘
```

Figure 1

Prioritizing objectives

Most managers would consider themselves very lucky indeed if they were required to focus on just one objective at a time. For most people, the reality is quite different. Where you are faced with a number of different objectives which all require attention, you need to find a way to establish which objectives and tasks:

- require immediate attention
- require attention fairly soon
- will require attention in the near future
- can be dealt with at some time, or can be delegated

PRIORITIZING USING THE URGENT OR IMPORTANT APPROACH

Each objective or task with which you are faced will fall into one of the following categories (Figure 2):

Priority 1 Urgent **and** Important	Priority 2 Important **but not** Urgent	Priority 3 Urgent **but not** Important	Priority 4 **Neither** Important nor Urgent
A key management task which is closely related to a high-level objective, and which has a fast-approaching deadline	A key management task which is closely related to a high-level objective	A task which has a fast-approaching deadline	A task which is not closely related to a high-level objective, and which does not have a fast-approaching deadline

Figure 2

ACTIVITY 11

Think about the objectives with which you have to deal at work. In this context, how would you define the difference between urgent and important? From your own experience, give one example for each of the categories listed below:

1 An example of a Priority 1 Urgent and Important objective would be:

2 An example of a Priority 2 Important but not Urgent objective would be:

3 An example of a Priority 3 Urgent but not Important objective would be:

4 An example of a Priority 4 objective that is neither Urgent nor Important would be:

FEEDBACK

Here are some examples of the way in which objectives can be prioritized according to Urgency and/or Importance.

Priority 1 Urgent and Important

- Install new computer system by end of next month
- Review all customer accounts by end of next week

Priority 2 Important but not Urgent

- Organize sales conference for next April
- Conduct staff appraisals by next January

Priority 3 Urgent but not Important

- Contract new window cleaning firm by next week
- Re-organize staff car parking spaces by Monday

Priority 4 Neither Urgent nor Important

- Review canteen menus
- Assess performance of current stationery supplier

PRIORITIZING USING THE ABC APPROACH

An alternative technique for prioritizing objectives is the *ABC approach*. You can use this to organize your list into three categories:

- **Category A**: This is the highest priority and simply cannot wait
- **Category B**: Must be done soon
- **Category C**: Can wait to be done after A and B, or could be delegated

An ABC list might look something like this:

(A) Update health and safety procedures

(A) Make presentation to the Board regarding new sales opportunities in Eastern Europe

(B) Negotiate marketing budget

(B) Design corporate logo

(C) Evaluate sales training programme

(C) Investigate Internet providers (delegate to Steve)

ACTIVITY 12   C3.2

1   Begin by listing your own work-related short-term objectives. Focus on those objectives which you need to achieve within the next three to six months.

2   Now prioritize your list, using either the Urgent/Important approach or the ABC approach.

Further on in this section we will be looking at how you can review progress to see whether or not the list needs to be updated.

PRIORITIZING LONG-TERM OBJECTIVES USING THE PAIRED COMPARISON APPROACH

When considering a list of long-term objectives sometimes the *Paired Comparison approach* is most useful. This is done by creating a matrix of all the objectives, then ranking each objective against all the others.

Say, for example, you are a Human Resources Manager who needs to prioritize the following objectives:

- implementing a staff appraisal system
- updating the staff employment handbook
- organizing redundancy arrangements for 2 per cent of the workforce
- introducing a flexible working system for office staff
- reviewing the company pension arrangements

Using Paired Comparison you would compare each objective with the others on the list and award points for importance. For example:

1   Compare **staff appraisal** with **updating the handbook**
    Award staff appraisal 2 points (appraisal is much more important than the handbook)
    Award updating the handbook 0 points (handbook is much less important than appraisal)

2   Compare **staff appraisal** with **organizing redundancy arrangements for 2 per cent of the workforce**
    Award staff appraisal 0 points (as it is much less important than redundancy)
    Award redundancy arrangements 2 points (as this is much more important than appraisal)

3   Compare **staff appraisal** with **introducing flexible working**
    Award staff appraisal 1 point (as it is equally as important as flexible working)
    Award introducing flexible working 1 point (as it is equally as important as appraisal)

At the end of the exercise, each objective will have a score which can then be compared with the other scores. An example of a completed Paired Comparison chart is shown in Figure 3.

	Appraisal	Handbook	Redundancy	Flexible working	Company pension
Appraisal		0	1	1	0
Handbook	2		2	2	1
Redundancy	0	0		1	0
Flexible working	1	0	2		0
Company pension	1	1	2	1	
Totals	4	1	7	5	1

Figure 3   Prioritizing using Paired Comparisons

The Paired Comparison chart shows that the priorities for this objective works out as:

- **First** priority: Redundancy arrangements (score 7)
- **Second** priority: Flexible working (score 5)
- **Third** priority: Appraisal system (score 4)
- **Joint fourth** priority: Handbook and company pension
                          (both score 1)

Reviewing progress

Once SMART objectives have been defined, you know precisely what you want to achieve. Undertaking regular reviews will enable you to check how you are doing and, where necessary, make adjustments. This process is shown in Figure 4.

- Identify what needs to be done

- Clarify the objective so that it meets the SMART criteria

- Organize information and determine:
  - what you already know
  - what you need to find out

- Create an action plan:
  - analyse the individual tasks which together, when completed, will enable you to achieve your objective
  - set a target date for completion of each task
  - prioritize tasks
  - decide which tasks are your sole responsibility and which tasks can be delegated
  - identify the resources needed
  - obtain the resources and, where necessary, allocate them appropriately

- Start work

- Regularly monitor progress against the completion dates:
  - are individual tasks completed by the dates which have been set?
  - are there sufficient resources? If not, what else do we need?

- Where necessary, take remedial action to ensure that completion dates will be met:
  - do I need to do anything extra?
  - do I need to recruit more people to the team, or delegate more tasks?
  - what else needs to be done to solve the problems or overcome the delays?

- Achieve the objective and evaluate and review the results:
  - what went well?
  - what caused difficulties?
  - how did I deal with the difficulties?
  - in the future, what will I do differently?
  - what have I learned from this?

Figure 4   The process of working towards an objective and evaluating whether or not you are on course for success

The next activity will give you an opportunity to reflect back on a project and evaluate how successful you were in achieving your objective.

ACTIVITY 13   C2, C3

Think about an objective which you have achieved in the recent past, and then answer the following questions:

1   What was your objective?

2   Did this objective meet the SMART criteria? yes ❑   no ❑

3   Did you identify, on paper, the individual tasks necessary for achievement of your objective? yes ❑   no ❑

4   Did you prioritize the tasks? yes ❑   no ❑

5   Which technique did you use to prioritize the tasks?

6   Did you set a completion date for each task? yes ❑   no ❑

7   What method did you use to monitor progress?

8   How often did you monitor progress?

9   Was it necessary to take action of some kind to ensure that progress was speeded up so that you could be sure of meeting some of the task completion dates? yes ❑   no ❑

10 What action did you take?

11 What was the result of the action you took?

12 Did you achieve your objective on time? yes ❑   no ❑

13 If not, why not?

14 What did you learn from this experience?

15 How will you apply this to future projects?

FEEDBACK

Review and evaluation is a key task. Wise managers learn from experience, so, by reviewing your successes and difficulties, you will be able to identify those activities, attitudes and approaches which:

- could usefully be repeated in the future
- should be avoided at all costs

The smooth progress and successful completion of the cycle of:

(1) → → → →	(2) → → → →	(3) → → → →	(4) → → → →
Planning and prioritizing	Implementing	Monitoring	Reviewing and evaluating

depends on rigorous objective setting and prioritizing right at the start. Remember, if you don't know exactly where you are going or when you are supposed to arrive, the journey can be very confusing, expensive and, ultimately, disappointing.

Summary

- Objectives help us to:
    - define where we want to go
    - plan the route
    - check to see how close we are to our final destination
    - confirm that we have arrived
- The words *objectives*, *aims*, *targets*, *goals* or *outcomes* all mean the same thing and are completely interchangeable.
- Worthwhile objectives are SMART:
    - **Simple**: straightforward and easy to understand
    - **Measurable**: so that you can see whether or not you have achieved what you set out to achieve. A non-measurable objective would be: 'Write enough letters'. A measurable objective would be: 'Write **twenty** letters'
    - **Achievable**: because setting objectives which are unlikely to be achieved is a waste of time and effort
    - **Realistic**: external factors may mean that changes have to be made
    - **Time-related**: so that you can see the time-frame for achievement. An objective which is not time-related would be: 'Complete the arrangements for the annual conference'. An objective which is time-related would be: 'Complete the arrangements for the annual conference **by 28 July 1996**'.
- Planning involves:
    - clarifying the SMART objective

- organizing available information and obtaining the required information
- identifying the individual tasks involved and assigning a completion date to each
- prioritizing tasks into a logical sequence
- completing each task in turn
- achieving the SMART objective

- Prioritizing using the Urgent or Important approach:

  - **Priority 1: Urgent and important**

    A task which is closely related to a high-level objective and which has a fast-approaching deadline

  - **Priority 2: Important but not urgent**

    A task which is closely related to a high-level objective

  - **Priority 3: Urgent but not important**

    A task which has a fast-approaching deadline

  - **Priority 4: Neither important nor urgent**

    A task which is not related to a high-level objective, and which does not have a fast-approaching deadline

- Prioritizing using the ABC approach:

  - **Category A**: Highest priority and simply cannot wait
  - **Category B**: Must be done soon
  - **Category C**: Can wait to be done after A and B, or could be delegated

- Prioritizing long-term objectives using the Paired Comparison approach:

  - Objectives are listed
  - Each objective is compared with the other objectives on the list and awarded points, e.g.: objective (a) compared with objective (b) – award 3 points to (a) because it is much more important than (b); award 1 point to (b) because it is much less important than (a)
  - When all the comparisons have been made, total the number of points awarded to each objective
  - Highest-scoring objectives have the highest priority; lowest-scoring objectives have the lowest priority

- Monitoring progress will enable you to check, on a regular basis, whether you are on target for success or whether changes need to be made
- Review and evaluation (after the objective has been achieved) will enable you to think carefully about:

  - what has gone well and what has not gone well
  - which actions you might usefully repeat in the future
  - which actions you should avoid in the future
  - what you have learned from the experience

Section 3 Influencing your way to success

Introduction

Influencing skills can best be summed up as a toolkit of:

- *communication skills* – speaking, questioning and listening
- *selling skills* – describing benefits and handling objections
- *interpersonal skills* – creating rapport and good working relationships

In this section of the Workbook we shall be exploring each element of the 'influencing toolkit' so that you will be able to use these skills in a very practical way to achieve your objectives.

What are influencing skills?

As a manager, influencing people at work is a key part of your role. You may feel slightly uncomfortable with the idea that you have the power to *influence* others. Your perception may be that influencing involves, in some way, manipulation and the misuse of power.

We influence the people around us all the time, both at home and at work, whenever we attempt to:

- sell an idea, a plan or an approach
- persuade others to see our point of view
- convince others that our ideas will work
- 'win over' people to our way of thinking

Influencing is **not** about manipulation or misuse of power, but it **is** about:

- establishing and maintaining good working relationships so that other people are receptive to us and willing to consider our suggestions
- presenting ideas logically and persuasively (and always truthfully) so that others can understand and appreciate the value of our proposals

ACTIVITY 14

Think back over the past six months and identify an occasion when you influenced (or attempted to influence) people at work. Briefly describe the situation in the space below, and identify four skills you used as part of the influencing process.

Situation:

Skills:
1
2
3

4

FEEDBACK

Situations in which you may have sought to influence others to see things your way include:

- *suggesting new ideas*: perhaps new products or services or ways of working or doing business
- *introducing change*: perhaps new systems, procedures, processes or approaches
- *requesting support*: perhaps for new projects or in conflict situations
- *requesting resources*: perhaps finance, equipment, space, staffing or time
- *requesting favours*: perhaps leave of absence or introductions to important contacts
- *requesting information or specialist knowledge*
- *negotiating or seeking a 'working compromise'*

The skills you may have used during the influencing process include:

- *Clarifying* objectives
  - being clear, in your own mind, about exactly what you want to achieve
- *Planning* the best way to achieve your objectives
  - what do I need to do? what do I need to say? which people do I need to see?
- *Organizing* and *presenting* information

- *Communicating* through speaking, listening, summarizing, questioning and the use of positive body language
- *Establishing* and *maintaining* positive relationships

Creating an influencing strategy

1 KNOW PRECISELY WHAT YOU WANT TO ACHIEVE

Before you can begin to create an influencing strategy you need to clarify what it is you want to achieve. This is your influencing objective, and it might be something like:

New idea:
- Sell the Board the idea that we should add Sweet and Sour Lobster to our range of packet soups

Change:
- Persuade the Training Department to change from training room seminars to a flexible learning/multi-media approach for delivery of customer care training in the retail outlets

Support:
- Convince Alison that she should support my findings (against likely strong opposition) at the team meeting when I suggest we abandon work on research project Fortune 10

Resources:
- Convince Tom that we need an immediate 20 per cent increase in the advertising budget

Favours:
- Convince Linda and her team that I'm the person who should go to New York to research market opportunities

Information and specialist knowledge:
- Persuade Vic to share his market research data with me before the Board meeting, so that I can prepare a report which recommends we go ahead with 'Plan B'

Negotiating or seeking a 'working compromise':
- Persuade the union, finance department and staff aged over 50 that my proposed early retirement package is the best option for everyone

2 PLAN YOUR CAMPAIGN

Once you know what you want to achieve, you need to consider the best way to present your case. Ask yourself:

- Who is involved?
- How will my proposals affect each of those individuals?
- What are the advantages and benefits for:
  - the individuals?
  - their team, department or function?
  - the company as a whole?
- What are their objections most likely to be?
- How should I deal with these objections? (What evidence can I present to show that the benefits of my proposal are real?)

3 COMMUNICATE YOUR IDEAS AND PROPOSALS

The way in which you communicate your ideas will have a direct bearing on whether or not you are successful. Ask yourself:

- Which is best:
  - one-to-one meetings?
  - team meetings?
  - a formal presentation?
  - a written report?
  - some combination of the above

Establishing the level of opposition

Whenever you are seeking to influence someone to do something, agree to something or see your point of view, they will generally hold one of the four positions shown in Figure 5 below.

Position −10	Position −5	Position 0	Position +5	Position +10
When someone is at position −10 they are diametrically opposed to your point of view. They have no sympathy whatsoever with your position and do **not** want to help or see things your way	When someone is at position -5 they have some major objections, but are not opposed to you 'on principle', in the same way as people at position −10	When someone is at position 0 they are neutral about you and your request. They have no strong feelings either way. Make a good case, and they can be persuaded and convinced	When someone is at position +5 they have some reservations, but generally feel fairly positive towards your ideas and approach	When someone is at position +10 they totally agree with your ideas and point of view and support you wholeheartedly

Figure 5   The starting positions of the people you are seeking to influence

ACTIVITY 15

Think back to the last time you used your influence at work to achieve a specific outcome. What were the levels of support and opposition at the beginning of your influencing strategy? To what extent had these levels of support and opposition changed by the end of your campaign? Complete the chart below by:

- noting down the name of each person you were hoping to influence
- marking on the chart the position of each person when you began your influencing strategy
- marking on the chart the position of each person when you had concluded your strategy

The completed chart will show you to what extent you managed to influence the people involved.

	Position −10	Position −5	Position 0	Position +5	Position +10
	Absolutely opposed	Major objections, but open to persuasion	Neutral	Some reservations, but generally positive	Very positive and offering total support
Person: Position when you commenced your strategy: Position when you completed your strategy:					
Person: Position when you commenced your strategy: Position when you completed your strategy:					
Person: Position when you commenced your strategy: Position when you completed your strategy:					
Person: Position when you commenced your strategy: Position when you completed your strategy:					

FEEDBACK

At the start of any influencing strategy it is always a good idea to work out, on paper, what people's positions are likely to be. This will help you to understand the level of opposition you are likely to face, and the amount of support you are likely to command.

Even if you have excellent influencing skills, it is very unlikely that you will be able to move someone from a −10 (diametrically opposed) position to a +10 (thinks your proposal is great) position. You should aim to move people two places to the right by the time you have concluded your strategy. In practice, this would mean:

- −10 people are transformed into people who are neutral to your ideas, but can be convinced
- −5 people, who have major objections at the start, become +5 people who still have some reservations, but who are, on the whole, positive
- neutral people and +5 people become very positive and supportive

ACTIVITY 16

There are a number of ways in which you can influence people to change their position from a minus to a plus. In the space below, list five things you can do to encourage someone to view you and your proposals in a positive light.

1

2

3

4

5

FEEDBACK

You can help to change a negative attitude to a positive attitude by:

- *Creating rapport* through:

    making it clear, through what you say and do, that you respect and understand the other person's position and point of view
    - behaving ethically (keeping conversations confidential, avoiding gossip and rumour, sticking to the truth even if it doesn't advance your cause, observing lines of authority and communication, playing fair and above-board)
    - maintaining your composure (adopting a calm, even and pleasant attitude, no matter how rattled or irritated you might actually feel)!

Techniques for assertiveness and stress management are dealt with in Workbook 2 of this series, *Managing Yourself*

- *Communicating effectively* by:
    - listening carefully and actively
    - using open and positive body language
    - asking the right kinds of questions
    - answering questions thoroughly and honestly
    - allowing the other person to openly voice his opinions and have his say
- *Presenting a strong case* by:
    - presenting the facts one point at a time, and in a logical order
    - avoiding jargon and too much detail (people don't like to be swamped with facts or data)
    - spelling out the benefits of your proposal, paying particular attention to any benefits which the target individual or group will enjoy if your proposal is adopted (This is what's in it for **you!**)

- dealing with objections calmly and reasonably
- checking to make sure that your proposal is thoroughly understood

Creating rapport

Your ability to create rapport and good working relationships with colleagues will have a direct bearing on the extent to which you are able to influence those people. Establishing good working relationships doesn't happen overnight. Within any organization there will be people with whom you get along really well, people with whom you have a fairly neutral relationship and others with whom you experience what might best be described as *relationship difficulties*. This is perfectly normal. The key point here is that your ability to influence people is, to a large extent, linked to the way in which people perceive you. The relationship between perceptions and willingness to be influenced is shown in Figure 6.

If you are perceived as	People will respond by
Someone who: ■ is fair, reasonable and honest ■ has a genuine concern for other people's feelings and points of view	■ being prepared to listen to your point of view and proposals
Someone who: ■ is arrogant, unreasonable and economical with the truth ■ has little regard for other people's opinions or concerns	■ being unwilling to be influenced by you

Figure 6   How people's perceptions of you will affect your ability to extend your influence

If you can:

- increase the number of **good** working relationships
- convert the **neutral** to **good**
- decrease the number of **difficult** relationships by converting them, at the least, to **neutral**

then you will expand your sphere of influence accordingly.

I WIN/YOU WIN

One important technique you can use to improve the way you are perceived and, consequently, improve relationships at work is the *win/win approach*.

ACTIVITY 17

For the purpose of this activity, consider each of the following scenarios and answer the accompanying questions.

Scenario 1

A colleague visits your office to discuss a matter which is of considerable importance to her and to ask for resources which only you can authorize. The meeting does not go well and, within a short space of time, you find yourself involved in a heated discussion. Your colleague, one way and another, gets the better of you, and you find yourself pushed into agreeing to her demands. When she leaves your office, you feel as though she has really taken advantage of the situation and that you have been manipulated into a losing position.

1 How might these events affect your opinion of this person?

2 How do you think you might respond to a request for help from this person in the future?

Scenario 2

A colleague visits your office to discuss a matter which is of considerable importance to her and to ask for resources which only you can authorize. The meeting does not go well and, within a short space of time, you find yourself involved in a heated discussion. You don't feel inclined to give way to her demands and you present some very clever arguments to show why, in this situation, you know best. When she leaves your office, you feel satisfied that you have won the argument and firmly 'put her in her place'.

1 How might these events affect this person's opinion of you?

2 How do you think this person might respond to a request for help from you in the future?

Scenario 3

A colleague visits your office to discuss a matter which is of considerable importance to her and to ask for resources which only you can authorize. The meeting does not go well and, within a short space of time, you find yourself involved in a heated discussion. The discussion quickly escalates into a full-blown shouting match and you both lose your tempers. She storms out, and you're upset and extremely angry. It feels to you as though you have both lost the argument.

1 How might these events affect the way in which you and your colleague could work together in the future?

2 How do you think each of you might respond to a request for help from the other?

I might feel:

She might feel:

Scenario 4

A colleague visits your office to discuss a matter which is of considerable importance to her and to ask for resources which only you can authorize. With your colleague you look for ways in which, together, you can achieve some kind of compromise. After some discussion and negotiation you work out a solution which allows both of you to obtain something positive from the situation. She feels as though the meeting was worthwhile, and so do you.

1 How might these events affect the way in which you and your colleague could work together in the future?

2 How do you think each of you might respond to a request for help from the other?

I might feel:

She might feel:

FEEDBACK

Most situations have one of four possible outcomes:

- You win/I lose
- I win/You lose
- I lose/you lose
- I win/You win

Each outcome has a very specific effect on the way in which the people involved perceive each other. These effects are shown in Figure 7.

You win/I lose	I win/You lose
You get the better of me and I feel irritated, frustrated, angry and upset. I feel very negative towards you and it will be unlikely that I shall want to help you in the future. In addition, I'll make sure that I **win** next time.	I get the better of you and so you feel irritated, frustrated, angry and upset. You feel negative towards me and will be unlikely to offer help or support in the future if I need it. In addition, you'll take whatever opportunity you can to make sure that **you win** next time.
I lose/You lose	**I win/You win**
We **both** feel irritated, frustrated, angry and upset and very negative towards one another. Neither of us really wants to work together in the future, and we'll do our best to stay out of each other's way. On the other hand, if we do have to collaborate in the future, then **we're both determined to win next time.**	Because we worked together and helped one another to each obtain something positive, we both feel pleased with the outcome. We can obviously work together to our mutual advantage and **we both look forward to further working opportunities in the future. We know we can both benefit.**

Figure 7

There are numerous practical ways in which you can demonstrate, in almost every situation, that you are keen to achieve a win/win outcome.

ACTIVITY 18

List six ways in which you can demonstrate to colleagues, in one-to-one and group situations, that you are actively seeking a win/win outcome.

1

2

3

4

5

6

FEEDBACK

You can show others that you are actively seeking a win/win outcome by:

Always

- respecting people as individuals and not 'pulling rank' or abusing your authority
- being honest if you don't have all the facts, or if you've made a mistake
- acknowledging that your viewpoint may be different, but also acknowledging that you **understand** the other's point of view
- making a genuine effort to explore possibilities that could lead to everyone gaining **something** from the situation (even if it is a compromise, rather than an ideal solution)

Never

- lying, blustering or losing your temper in an attempt to intimidate people
- judging, criticizing and nit-picking
- jumping to conclusions before you've heard the whole story
- keeping a closed mind because you're convinced that you are right
- withholding necessary information
- using unethical tactics to get your own way and 'win'

Hearing, understanding, agreeing, taking action

When you seek to influence someone to accept your proposals, you need to bear in mind four key objectives. You need the people who are on the receiving end of your influencing message to:

- **hear** your message
- **understand** your message
- **agree with** your message
- **take the action you want**

Use the next activity as an opportunity to think about what could prevent you from achieving these key influencing objectives.

ACTIVITY 19

1 List three reasons why people might not **hear** your message:

1

2

3

2 List three reasons why people might not **understand** your message:

1

2

3

3 List three reasons why people may be unable to **agree** with your message:

1

2

3

4 List three reasons why people may resist **taking the action you want them to take**:

1

2

3

| FEEDBACK |

WHY PEOPLE MAY NOT HEAR YOUR MESSAGE

Although someone may **listen** to your message (or read your report), there are a number of reasons why they may not **hear** what you are saying. These reasons may be that they:

- have their own agenda, which is very different to yours
- feel that your proposals are not in their best interest
- do not recognize the importance of your proposals
- are not convinced that you have considered all the implications of your proposals
- make assumptions based on past experience (they 'switch off' because they think they've heard it all before and they didn't like it then, so why should they like it now?)
- jump to conclusions halfway through and stop listening

WHY PEOPLE MAY NOT UNDERSTAND YOUR MESSAGE

As the communicator, it is your responsibility to present your message (either verbally or in writing) so that your audience can understand. People may be unable to understand your proposal because your message:

- is incomplete
- is muddled or unclear
- is not presented in a logical sequence
- does not spell out the benefits
- is loaded with jargon or technical/scientific/numerical data

WHY PEOPLE MAY NOT BE PREPARED TO AGREE

When attempting to influence others, you may find yourself running into the 'Oh, I don't know, I'm not sure. I need to give this some thought and get back to you' syndrome. People may be unwilling to commit to your proposal because they:

- feel threatened
- feel overwhelmed by your persuasiveness (this can happen if you *oversell* an idea)
- wonder:
    - what's in it for you?
    - what's in it for me?
    - if you win, will I lose?
- worry in case their agreement will be perceived as a 'climb-down' from a previously held position
- want to find out what 'everyone else' thinks before they commit themselves

WHY PEOPLE MAY RESIST TAKING THE ACTION YOU WANT THEM TO TAKE

Sometimes people may recognize that your proposals make good sense, yet they still hold back from taking the necessary action. For example:

- You want to introduce 360-degree feedback, but the Human Resources Manager is resisting
- You want to re-design the packaging for Product ABC, but the marketing team are resisting
- You want to introduce internal electronic mail, but the MD is resisting
- You want to introduce a results related incentive scheme, but everyone is resisting

Fear is a very strong emotion. Quite simply, you may fail to influence people to take the action you are suggesting because they fear the consequences:

- 'What if it all goes wrong?'
- 'If I agree, will I be making a big mistake?'
- 'Will it make matters even worse than they are now?'
- 'If I go along with this, how will other people perceive me?
- 'This means change ... and I don't like change.'
- 'Maybe I won't be able to cope.'
- 'I hate making decisions ... let's leave things the way they are, and maybe everything will just work out.'

Communicating effectively

Effective communication is a key influencing skill because it is important that people **hear** and **understand** what you have to say. Regardless of whether you are seeking to influence just one person or a group of people, the way in which you communicate your ideas and proposals will have a powerful effect on the outcome.

ACTIVITY 20   C2, C3

Think back to a work situation in which you were keen to influence other people to agree and action your proposals. During the course of your influencing campaign you will have used a range of communication skills and behaviours to present your ideas. Which of those behaviours were most effective and useful? What, if anything, would you avoid doing in a similar situation in the future? Note down your ideas on the checklist below.

Useful and helpful communication behaviours	Unhelpful communication behaviours I will avoid in the future
■ *Effective listening:*	■ *Ineffective listening:*
■ *Effective speaking:*	■ *Ineffective speaking:*
■ *Effective questioning*	■ *Ineffective questioning*
■ *Effective non-verbal 'body language':*	■ *Ineffective non-verbal 'body language':*
■ *Effective written communication:*	■ *Ineffective written communication:*

FEEDBACK

The most effective techniques for persuading people to hear what you have to say are:

- actively listening to what **they** have to say
- asking the right kinds of questions to find out their real concerns
- using open and friendly body language to communicate, without words, your good intentions
- pitching your proposals at the right level – neither condescending and patronizing, nor too technical
- using the right medium – for example, one-to-one meeting, telephone call, letter, formal group presentation

The checklist you completed in response to the previous activity may look something like this:

Useful and helpful communication behaviours	Unhelpful communication behaviours I will avoid in the future

■ *Effective Listening:*
  – paying close attention to the words
  – paying close attention to the emotions behind the words
  – listening for unspoken messages
  – showing that you value the other person's views and opinions by allowing the speaker to have his or her say (even if it takes forever!)
  – summarizing what has been said so that you are sure you understand:
'So, it seems to me that your main concern is …'
 	
■ *Effective Speaking:*
  – getting to the point and sticking to the point
	■ *Ineffective listening:*
	  – allowing yourself to be distracted by your own thoughts, noise, the speaker's appearance or mannerisms
	  – interrupting or 'talking over' the speaker
	  – assuming you know what is coming next and beginning to formulate a response, mentally, while the speaker is still speaking
	  – ignoring concerns which have been stated in the hope that they will just go away
	
	■ *Ineffective speaking:*
	  – using jargon or *buzz-words* in an attempt to impress
	  – talking fast or loudly in an attempt to intimidate

Useful and helpful communication behaviours	Unhelpful communication behaviours I will avoid in the future
– actually saying that you agree with the other person, if you do (Everyone likes to hear 'I agree absolutely' and 'Yes, you're right!) – matching the speed and volume of your speech to your listener's speech – using vocabulary your speaker will understand – avoiding repetition and unnecessary detail	– using sarcasm or inappropriate humour – showing aggression by shouting or swearing – showing submission by constantly apologizing
■ *Effective questioning*: – using *open questions* which begin with How? Why? What? Where? When? which require the other person to give a fairly detailed answer: 'If you were in my position, how would you tackle it?' 'How do you see it?' 'What alternatives would you suggest? 'What is the key issue for you?	■ *Ineffective questioning*: – using *closed questions* which can be answered with a simple Yes or No: 'Do you agree?' 'Can you see the sense of what I'm saying?' 'Will you support me on this?' 'Is there anything else I can say?'
■ *Effective non-verbal 'body language'*: – maintaining eye contact for roughly 60 per cent of the time, but making sure you don't stare – maintaining a professional distance from others, and not attempting to invade personal space	■ *Ineffective non-verbal 'body language'*: – avoiding eye contact by looking at the floor, out of the window, etc. – shuffling papers, surreptitious watch-checking, finger tapping or other signs of irritation or impatience

Useful and helpful communication behaviours	Unhelpful communication behaviours I will avoid in the future
– sitting or standing easily, and appearing to be calm, relaxed and in control	– showing aggression by table-thumping, finger pointing, throwing papers around – showing lack of confidence by slouching or mannerisms like nail biting or pencil chewing
■ *Effective written communication:* – recognizes the value of people's time, and should be brief and to the point – contains the essential facts and relevant detail – is subdivided into small sections or chapters so that people can read, absorb and understand the material – uses normal language and the minimum of jargon and statistics	■ Ineffective written communication: – assumes that people have the time and the desire to read yet another 40-page report – is hastily prepared and ill-considered – contains data, statistics and information which is generally meaningless to a non-specialist – is used when the communicator can't be bothered to set up a meeting

Presenting a strong case

Effective communication will enable people to **hear** and **understand** your arguments and point of view. To help people to **agree** and **take the action you require**, you need to be able to present a strong case for your proposal. This involves selling the benefits and dealing with objections.

SELLING THE BENEFITS

As part of the initial planning process, you need to identify (preferably on paper) exactly how your proposal will benefit your supporters. For example:

1 Proposal made to the Board:

- We should add Sweet and Sour Lobster to our range of packet soups.

Benefits for the Board:

- Market Research has shown that this would be a popular flavour, *which means that we could increase our market share of packet soups by 5 per cent*
- The research lab has already produced a recipe, *which means that there wouldn't be any additional development costs*
- The packaging would require minimal changes, *so a change would be reasonably cost-effective*
- We have sufficient funds in the marketing budget to cover the cost of the campaign, *which means that we wouldn't be looking for additional money*
- We have spare capacity on line 12, so we could start a lobster run immediately, *which means that we could hit the Christmas market and reap the benefits of extra sales straight away*
- I understand JH Foods is coming on-line with a range of Mexican packet soups, *which means we need a new product so that we position ourselves competitively*
- I've prepared a marketing and sales campaign, *which means that if I get your approval today, we can move ahead straight away. This would be the only decision you need to make and there would be nothing else for you to do. It would be very straightforward from here.*

2 Proposal made to Alison:

- Support my findings (against likely strong opposition) at the team meeting when I suggest we abandon work on research project Fortune 10

Benefits for Alison

- We both know that Fortune 10 isn't going anywhere. Pulling the plug now *means that, in the long run, we're going to save the company a great deal of money. Carol will remember that **we** did that*
- If we abandon Fortune 10, *that means you'll have more time to spend on your bacteria project. You may even be able to get some additional funding as well*
- If you support me on this one, *I'll strongly recommend that Carol includes you in the Toronto team*

ACTIVITY 21

Consider an influencing strategy with which you are currently involved (or one that you have in mind for the near future), and complete the chart below.

Your influencing strategy objectives:	
People you need to influence	**How your strategy will benefit each person**

FEEDBACK

Clearly, your response to this activity will be individual to you and whatever you are hoping to achieve as a result. Even so, **every** influencing strategy has the following in common:

- an objective (desired outcome)
- one or more people who can assist you in achieving your desired outcome
- one or more benefits for each of the people involved

People generally want to know: *'What's in it for me?'* If you can show someone they will benefit as a result of helping you, they will be more likely to assist. This may seem cynical, but it is a fact of life. The key point here is that you need to define the benefits which others will enjoy, and then clearly spell them out, when you are asking for support.

OVERCOMING OBJECTIONS

People are motivated to raise objections through:

- fear
- habit
- misunderstanding

Fear

People raise objections because they are frightened that, if they go along with you, they will be making a mistake. For example:

Thinks: - 'I'm not sure he's thought this through. It could go very badly wrong'
- 'If this doesn't work, I could end up carrying the can for it'

Says: - 'I don't think it's the right time'
- 'I'm not convinced we need to do this'

Habit

People raise objections because they are reluctant to change. For example:

Thinks: - 'There's a lot of extra work involved'
- 'I'm comfortable with the way things are – maybe I won't be able to cope with a new approach'

Says: - 'The way we do it now seems to work'
- 'I don't see the need for change'

Misunderstanding

People raise objections because they don't really understand your proposals, but are reluctant to admit that they haven't grasped your strategy.

Thinks: - 'I don't really understand, so I'd better say no'
- 'None of this makes sense to me, so I'm agreeing to nothing!'

Says: - 'Seems like a complicated process'
- 'I think what we're doing now is fairly straightforward and gets results'

ACTIVITY 22

What is the best way to deal with objections which are based on fear, habit or misunderstanding?

1   The best way to overcome objections which are raised because of **fear** is to:

2   The best way to overcome objections which are raised because of **habit** is to:

3   The best way to overcome objections which are raised because of **misunderstanding** is to:

FEEDBACK

People who raise objections based on fear need reassurance. The best way to handle fear objections is to give examples of similar situations where the action you are proposing worked well. You may need to do some research, and you should make sure that the facts you present which support your argument are honest and truthful. Don't be tempted to skew the information in your favour. If people can see that similar propositions have worked in other companies, they will feel reassured and encouraged.

Where you find yourself having to deal with habit objections, you will get the best results by emphasizing the benefits which the individual will experience if your plan goes ahead. Many people resist new ideas because 'it's easier to resist than to change'. Show them how the change will bring benefits which they, personally, will enjoy.

Misunderstanding objections can easily be handled by re-stating your arguments simply, clearly and logically. Sometimes it will be helpful to put your ideas in writing because, for some people, new concepts which are presented on paper are easier to understand than information which is presented verbally.

The next activity will give you an opportunity to chart your progress as you proceed with an influencing strategy.

ACTIVITY 23

This activity will enable you to:

(a) define your strategy and the level of opposition or support you can expect
(b) record your progress
(c) measure your success

Part A: To be completed before you start

1 Proposed start date:

2 Expected completion date:

3 Influencing objective (specific outcome required)

4 People who are likely to offer support (+10 and +5 positions):

People who are likely to be neutral to my proposal:

People who are likely to be opposed (-5 and -10 positions):

5 Objections which are likely to be raised:

6 The ways in which I will overcome these objections:

Part B: To be completed halfway through your influencing project

1 People who have been moved from a minus to a neutral or plus position:

People who have been moved from a neutral to a plus position:

2 Unexpected challenges which have occurred:

Ways in which I have dealt with these:

3 Effective communication strategies I have used:

4 Additional comments:

Part C: To be completed at the end of your influencing project

1 Outcome, and how this compares to my original objective:

2 Specific learning points:

Actions I will repeat in the future:

Actions I will avoid in the future:

3 Additional comments:

Summary

- You use influencing skills when you:
  - suggest new ideas
  - introduce change
  - request support, resources, favours, information or specialist knowledge
  - negotiate or seek a 'working compromise'
- When creating an influencing strategy, you need to:
  - know precisely what it is you want to achieve
  - plan your campaign
  - communicate your ideas and proposals
- Each situation has four possible outcomes:
  - **You win**/I lose … so next time I'll make sure that I win, just to even the score
  - **I win**/You lose … so next time, you make sure you win … no matter what it takes
  - **I lose/You lose** … we're both pretty angry and upset … and we're both determined to win, next time
  - **I win/You win** … we both look forward to working together in the future because we know we can both benefit
- To show that you are looking for a win/win outcome:

  Do:

  - respect people as individuals
  - be honest – even if it means admitting you don't know all the answers, or that you've made a mistake
  - demonstrate that, even if you don't agree, at least you understand the other person's point of view
  - explore all possibilities with an open mind

  Don't:
  - attempt to intimidate people by shouting, lying or exercising your power (as a senior colleague or the person with money to spend)
  - judge or criticize
  - jump to conclusions
  - withhold information
  - use unethical tactics to win
- The key objectives of any influencing strategy are to get other people to:
  - hear your message
  - understand your message
  - agree with your message

- take the action you want them to take
- Presenting a strong case involves selling the benefits. This means identifying the ways in which your listener will benefit from your proposal, and answering the unspoken question: 'What's in it for me?'
- Identifying and overcoming objections:
  - handling **fear** objections by providing reassurance and giving examples of similar situations where your proposed action worked well
  - handling **habit** objections by showing your listener how your proposal will bring personal benefits for them
  - handling **misunderstanding** objections by explaining your plans logically and simply – as many times as necessary – so that your listener is absolutely clear about what you want to do

Section 4 Decisions, decisions!

Introduction

Regardless of how you feel about making decisions, whether you relish or loathe them, decision making is another key management task from which there is no escape. In this section we will be looking at your personal decision-making style and exploring, in detail, the decision-making cycle.

What's your style?

For most managers, their working lives seem to consist of one long round of decisions which have to be made. Sometimes they are simple, straightforward decisions: 'Do you want to see Michelle now, or shall I ask her to call back?', and sometimes they are very complex and difficult decisions: 'We've lost the German contract and the bank is threatening to call in the overdraft. What are we going to do?' or 'Simon's going to take us to an Industrial Tribunal for unfair dismissal, but the MD says we can't risk any bad press – what are we going to do?'

A decision usually involves making a choice between alternatives. Most people have a particular style or approach which they use to select the alternative which they feel, under the circumstances, will produce the best results.

ACTIVISTS

Activists are keen to get on with the decision-making process.

- 'The main thing is, let's make a decision ... if it's wrong, we'll make another one – fast!'

REFLECTORS

Reflectors like to take their time, analyse the situation and explore all the possibilities before committing themselves to action:

■ 'Let's look at the problem, talk it through, think about it carefully – we don't want to rush into anything until we're sure we've got it right.'

THEORISTS

Theorists need to have all the facts before they choose. Unless they have the complete picture, they feel they are unable to make a sensible decision.

■ 'How can I decide to go ahead if it has never been done before? You can't expect me to make a decision until I know what the outcome is going to be!'

PRAGMATISTS

Pragmatists like to make links between what they have learned and the job in hand:

■ 'That's an interesting idea ... I wonder if it would work in an office as well?'

ACTIVITY 24

I   Read through each of the descriptions above and identify which, in most circumstances, is your preferred decision-making style.

Tick one box only

(a) Generally, I would describe myself as an Activist when
     making decisions   ❑

(b) Generally, I would describe myself as a Reflector when
     making decisions   ❑

(c) Generally, I would describe myself as a Theorist when
     making decisions   ❑

(d) Generally, I would describe myself as a Pragmatist when
     making decisions   ❑

2   Identify the main drawback for each of these four approaches to decision making:

(a) The main drawback to using the Activist approach is:

(b) The main drawback to using the Reflector approach is:

(c) The main drawback to using the Theorist approach is:

(d) The main drawback to using the Pragmatist approach is:

FEEDBACK

If, in response to the previous activity, you identified yourself as an Activist, you recognized that you tend to jump in with an instant solution, often basing your choice on past experience. You prefer to make **some** decision rather than **no** decision at all.

CASE STUDY

Charlie, Training Manager with a merchant bank:

The disadvantage of always taking an activist approach was brought home to me in a big way quite recently. I had to make a decision about out-sourcing some training ... who was going to get the contract? I'd used a consultancy for similar work in the past so, without much thought, I decided to use them again. It had worked before, I thought, so it would work again. It was a disaster – the consultants didn't have the range of skills we needed because the task was much more complex. I jumped in with both feet – and I got burned! More analysis and less haste in the future, I think.

If you believe that, generally, you could be described as someone who approaches decision making as a Reflector, then you will have identified that you take a long time to choose between alternatives. Sometimes you may need to prod yourself into action to avoid the 'analysis/paralysis' trap.

CASE STUDY

Simone, Senior Partner in an accountancy practice:

I have to take an analytical approach to life – that's what my job is about. It's also the way my mind works. I like to analyse, discuss, compare … and I drive the other partners crazy sometimes, I know that. Some months ago we were looking at a new corporate image for our stationery, and I felt it was very important to get it right. Everyone else had made a decision and I held everything up because I wanted to compare our options with what other similar companies were using. And I wanted to make sure we were going to get the best price deal, combined with the best quality. It wasn't that I couldn't make a decision, I just wanted to make the right decision. The delay cost the firm a considerable amount of money because we lost out on a 35 per cent discount deal which another partner had negotiated. I was not flavour-of-the-month with our practice manager, and I don't think my partners were too pleased, either.

If you consider yourself to be a Theorist, then you may need to come to terms with the fact that decisions often have to be made on the basis of incomplete data and that intuition sometimes has a role to play.

CASE STUDY

Neville, Production Manager with a food manufacturing company:

We wanted to get in on the ground floor with a new snack food. The problem was that the machinery we needed was manufactured in Germany, and if we bought it we'd have to change the specification to meet our needs. But I didn't know the extent of the changes we might have to make. I couldn't go to Germany to have a look because our Head Office in the US wanted the new product kept under wraps until the marketing started. It was my decision whether to buy from Germany and hope we could convert, or wait nine months until a UK manufacturer could produce exactly what we wanted. How could I make a decision about something I'd never seen? If the German machinery was terribly wrong, it was going to cost a fortune to put right. If I waited, we could lose a big slice of the market. How are you supposed to choose between two options like that?

If you decided that you are a Pragmatist, then you will understand how you are able to make connections between apparently unrelated topics and then try them out to see if they work.

CASE STUDY

Liam, Senior Design Manager with a software design company:

We recently discovered a major design problem with a software system we had created for a new and very important client. None of our designers could sort out the problem, and time was running out – the client was waiting for the product. I remembered a technique I'd learned on, of all things, an angling course I'd been on in Scotland. I made the connection between the 'fishing concept' and the design problem and decided to try it out to see if it would work. The design team couldn't figure out how I'd solved the problem so quickly ... and I didn't tell them!

The decision-making cycle

There are many, many kinds of decisions which managers have to make, including those which are:

- quite important, quite urgent, fairly straightforward:
  - 'What colour scheme shall we use for the reception area?'
  - 'Shall we set up a Home Page on the Internet?'
  - 'Shall we have the annual conference here, or in Surrey?'
- very important, urgent, fairly complex:
  - 'Is it time to change the packaging for our 'Colour Lite' hair product?'
  - 'Should we stick with a combined Human Resources and Training Department, or should we split the functions and appoint a Training Manager?'
  - 'Should we introduce Just in Time?'
- Extremely important, extremely urgent, very complex:
  - 'There's a toxic waste spillage at the Bolton plant – how can we contain the damage and what do we tell the media?'
  - 'There's a major design fault in the car which is due to be launched next week, how do we fix it?'
  - 'Three supermarkets report that our product has been tampered with and contaminated. How do we alert the public? How do we withdraw all stocks? How do we restore public confidence?'

No matter what the choices are, you will need to progress through a number of stages (the decision-making cycle) in order to reach the best possible decision in the time available.

ACTIVITY 25

Think back to the last important decision you made at work and then note down, in the space below, up to five steps you took which enabled you to move from:

- *Starting point of the decision-making cycle* ('I need to make a decision')

through to

- *Completion of the decision-making cycle* ('Good! Another decision made!')

Decision-making cycle

1

2

3

4

5

FEEDBACK

Figure 8 shows the five stages of the decision-making cycle.

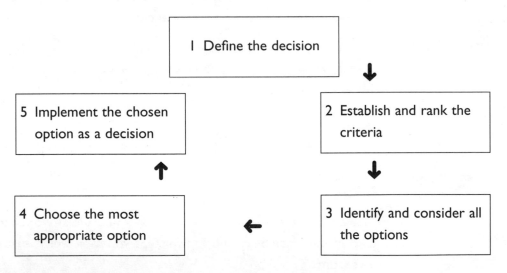

Figure 8   The decision-making cycle

DEFINE THE DECISION

Before you can find a solution, you need to be sure that you have clearly defined the problem and that you are aware of any additional, subsidiary decisions which may be required as a consequence of the first decision. For example:

Main decision:

- 'What colour scheme should we use for the reception area?'

might seem like a problem which requires just one simple decision. But it might also raise a number of additional issues which also require solutions and decisions. For example:

Subsidiary decisions:

- 'If we decorate the reception area, will the rest of the ground floor need to be decorated as well?'
- 'If we decorate, do we need to organize new carpet? If so, should we buy something reasonable but fairly cheap because we are planning to move? Or should we go for really good quality, so that when we relocate to our new offices we can take the carpet with us?'
- 'If we decide to, **can** we take the carpet with us – what does it say in the lease?'

and so on. The quantity or complexity of the subsidiary questions might actually cause you to ask:

- 'In view of the fact that we're relocating, do we really **need** to decorate the reception area?'

Once you have defined the decision, together with any subsidiary decisions, and concluded that this is a decision which really does need to be made, you can then move on to the next stage of the cycle.

ESTABLISH AND RANK THE CRITERIA

The criteria are the factors which you need to take into account when comparing the different options available. The criteria you set will influence your final choice.

Criteria can be:

- *Resources* criteria:
  - capital and running costs
  - time constraints
  - manpower and skill constraints
  - geographical and location constraints
- *Features* criteria:
  - *computers*: must have minimum of 1 gb hard disk space
  - *vehicles*: must be available with a lease option
  - *factory site*: must be situated with easy access to M25 and airports
  - *staff*: must be an Honours graduate with French as his/her first language

- *Outcome* criteria:

  Positive outcome criteria are the results that the decision maker wants the decision to produce, while negative outcome criteria are the results that the decision maker hopes to avoid.

  Positive outcome criteria which are required:
  - pleasant work environment
  - increase in market share
  - positive media reporting

  Negative outcome criteria which are to be avoided:
  - delays in project completion
  - dissatisfied customers
  - loss of competitive advantage

Say, for example, that you have to make a decision about which Internet service provider to choose. You have defined the decision and you're absolutely sure that it is a decision which needs to be made. The criteria against which you measure the available options might be:

A service provider which:

Resources criteria:

- charges a set monthly fee with no additional access costs
- offers local telephone charges at the access points

Features criteria:

- uses 28,000 baud modem so that information is transferred quickly
- provides free Web space so that we can set up a Home Page
- provides a comprehensive customer helpline facility

Positive outcomes criteria:

- is compatible with the provider used by our Hamburg office, so we can transfer files by e-mail

Once you have established your criteria, the next task is to rank the chosen criteria in order of importance to you at that moment in time. There is no right or wrong way to do this. You will rank the criteria according to internal and external circumstances, your individual needs, and the needs of your organization. For example, you might rank the above criteria as follows:

1 Is compatible with the provider used by our Hamburg office, so we can transfer files by e-mail
2 Charges a set monthly fee with no additional access costs
3 Offers local telephone charges at the access points
4 Uses 28,000 baud modem for fast transferral of information

5   Provides free Web space so that we can set up a Home Page

6   Provides a comprehensive customer helpline facility

or as follows:

1   Charges a set monthly fee with no additional access costs

2   Offers local telephone charges at the access points

3   Provides free Web space so that we can set up a Home Page

4   Uses 28,000 baud modem for fast transferral of information

5   Provides a comprehensive customer helpline facility

6   Is compatible with the provider used by our Hamburg office, so we can transfer files by e-mail

The next activity will give you an opportunity to identify the criteria which you need to apply to a current work-related decision, and to rank your chosen criteria in order of importance.

ACTIVITY 26

Think about a work-related decision which you face at the moment.

1   Note down the criteria which you will apply to each available option:

Resources:

Features:

Positive outcomes you want to achieve:

Negative outcomes you hope to avoid:

2   Rank your criteria in order of importance:

IDENTIFY AND CONSIDER ALL THE OPTIONS

Once you have identified the criteria you want to apply, and have ranked them according to importance, your next task is to find two or three options which match your list.

In an ideal world, you would be able to discover an option which is a perfect fit. For example, 'I need to decide which laser printer to buy ... I need the printer to match six specific criteria ... terrific, Santori Ltd make a machine which fits my needs perfectly .... that's the option I'll go for.'

Sadly, we don't live in an ideal world. Consequently, when decision making you will often find yourself having to choose between two or more less than ideal options.

CHOOSE THE MOST APPROPRIATE OPTION

Choosing the most appropriate option is the art of making the decision which will give you the results you want. As you will know from your own experience, sometimes this is a straightforward exercise, and sometimes it can be agonizing.

ACTIVITY 27

What system do you usually use to enable you to choose between alternative options? Describe the process (or processes) in the space below.

When faced with making a decision where I have to choose between two or more different options, I usually:

There are a number of techniques, involving judgement and analysis, which you can use to help you choose the option which will provide most, if not all, the benefits you are looking for. For each option you might use:

- **Simple cost-benefit analysis**
  - List the benefits and the disadvantages of each option
  - Analyse, for each option, which benefit or disadvantage outweighs all the others. For example: If 50 per cent of the workforce may have to be made redundant if option (1) is chosen, this alternative might well be immediately ruled out. Or if Option (2) requires a capital investment of £1.5 million, then this alternative could be dismissed straight away. Using analysis and judgement you can continue to narrow the field, eliminating unsuitable alternatives until, eventually, you are left with the most suitable option
- **Scenario planning**
  - For each possible alternative, run through the 'best-case' and 'worst-case' scenarios – 'What if …?' and 'But if then this happened …?' – so that you can get an overview of what could take place in the **future** as a direct result of the decision made **today**
- When faced with **equally** attractive options, **use your intuition**, which is a combination of:
  - past knowledge and experience of similar situations and similar people
  - a subconscious understanding of the nature, motivations and personalities of the other people involved
  - a subconscious understanding of what is likely to be the outcome, given all the factors involved

---

Nick, MD of a management consultancy, explains:

We were looking to expand into Europe and there were two offers on the table. When we considered them from every angle, they appeared to be absolutely equal. Any advantages we might have gained from creating a working partnership with option A were matched by option B, and vice versa.

Same with the disadvantages. You couldn't have put a pin between them, and I was absolutely stumped. Naturally I consulted the team but, as MD, the final decision was down to me, and I didn't know how to choose. In the end I went with my gut-feeling … instinct, intuition, whatever you want to call it. It's worked really well and I have no regrets ... but I don't know if it would have been even better if I'd gone with the other deal. Under the circumstances, there was no 'logical' system I could have used which would have helped me to make a better decision than the one I took.

In Workbook 15, *Making Rational Decisions,* you will have the opportunity to explore a number of sophisticated techniques for analysing information during the decision-making process.

IMPLEMENT THE CHOSEN OPTION AS A DECISION

This is the final step in the decision-making cycle. It is the point at which, having committed yourself to an option, you put your plan into action. This is when you need to:

- monitor what happens
- compare the reality with your expectations
- make adjustments to keep the decision on course for success
- keep your nerve if things appear to be going wrong
- be prepared to live with the consequences

It is important to recognize that, sometimes, you will make less than perfect decisions. Sometimes you will make decisions which have unforeseen consequences, and, if you are like most people, at some time in your career you will probably make a decision which, in retrospect and with the benefit of hindsight, will seem like a breathtaking example of poor judgement. The key points here are to make sure, when making decisions, that you:

- decide what you want to achieve
- gather the relevant information
- analyse the information
- make full use of whatever time is available
- use your knowledge, experience and skill to make the best possible decision under the prevailing circumstances

Summary

- People who make decisions using an **Activist** approach base current decisions on past experience. They also make decisions quickly, preferring **any** decision, rather than no decision at all
- **Reflectors** are slow to reach a decision because they like to have all the facts, and to weigh and analyse the information before finally deciding
- **Theorists** find it hard to make a decision unless they have **all** the facts — which, in real life, is not always possible
- **Pragmatists** are fairly experimental. They are able to make connections between apparently unrelated topics and then apply them to the decision-making process to see if they will work
- The five steps of the decision-making cycle are:
  - define the decision
  - establish and rank the criteria
  - identify and consider all the options
  - choose the most appropriate option
  - implement the chosen option as a decision
- The factors which you need to take into account when comparing different options are:
  - resources — e.g. capital and running costs, time, manpower, etc.
  - features — e.g. mobile phone must be digital; secretary must be familiar with Windows '95; office space must be air-conditioned.
  - outcomes:
  - this is the end result I want — e.g. increase in market share
  - this is the end result I do not want — e.g. increase in running costs
- **Cost-benefit analysis** technique involves:
  - listing the pros and cons of each option
  - analysing, for each option, which plus or minus point outweighs all the others — e.g If we do **this** it will cost £1 million — so forget it!
- **Scenario planning** technique involves:
  - working out the 'best-case' and 'worst-case' scenario for each option: 'If everything goes perfectly, this will happen. If everything that could go wrong **does** go wrong, this will happen'
- Implementing the chosen decision involves:
- monitoring what happens
- comparing what is actually happening with what you thought would happen
- making adjustments, if necessary
- keeping your nerve if things appear to be going wrong
- being prepared to live with the consequences of your decision

Summary

Now that you have completed the first Workbook in this series, you should feel confident that you have a sound grasp of:

- business ethics
- planning and prioritizing objectives
- influencing skills
- the importance of taking an analytical approach to decision making.

In Workbook 2, *Managing Yourself,* we will be exploring assertiveness techniques and looking at ways in which you can more effectively manage conflict, stress and time.

Topics which have been touched upon in this workbook are covered in greater depth in later books in this series:

- Workbook 7: *Leading from the Front*
- Workbook 9: *Project Management*
- Workbook 13: *Building a High Performance Team*
- Workbook 14: *The New Model Leader*
- Workbook 15: *Making Rational Decisions*
- Workbook 16: *Communication*

Recommended reading

Brigley, S. (1994) *Walking the Tightrope: A survey of ethics in management*, Institute of Management Research Report.

Codes of Ethics: Management Checklists, Checklist 028, Institute of Management Foundation.

The Effective Manager: managing people: managing yourself (1995), Pitman Publishing in association with the Institute of Management Foundation.

Introducing a Whistleblowing Policy; Management Checklists, Checklist 072: Institute of Management Foundation.

Dixon, R. (1997) *The Management Task*, Butterworth-Heinemann in association with the Institute of Management Foundation.

Murdock, A. and Scutt, C. (1993, repr. 1994, 1995) *Personal Effectiveness*, Butterworth-Heinemann in association with the Institute of Management Foundation.

Norton, B and Kelly, A. (1996) *Business Ethics: Management Directions*, Institute of Management Foundation.

Peel, M. (1995) *Successful Decision-Making in a Week*, Institute of Management Foundation/Hodder & Stoughton.

About the Institute of Management

The mission of the Institute of Management (IM) is to promote the development, exercise and recognition of professional management.

The IM is the leading professional organization for managers. Its efforts and resources are devoted to ensuring the continuing development and success of its members.

At the forefront of management standards, the IM provides a range of services for its members. These include flexible training programmes and a unique range of support services such as career counselling, enquiry and research facilities and preferential prices on IM publications and other IM products.

Further details about the Institute of Management may be obtained from:

Institute of Management
Management House
Cottingham Road
Corby
Northants
NN17 1TT

Telephone 01536 204222

We need your views

We really need your views in order to make the Institue of Management Open Learning Programme an even better learning tool for you. Please take time out to complete and return this questionnaire to Tessa Gingell, Pergamon Open Learning, Linacre House, Jordan Hill, Oxford OX2 8DP.

Name:...

Address:...

....

Title of workbook:...

If applicable, please state which qualification you are studying for. If not, please describe what study you are undertaking, and with which organization or college:

....

Please grade the following out of 10 (10 being extremely good, 0 being extremely poor):

Content: .... Suitability for ability level: ....

Readability: .... Qualification coverage: ....

What did you particularly like about this workbook?

....

Are there any features you disliked about this workbook? Please identify them.

....

Are there any errors we have missed?
If so, please state page number: ....

How are you using the material? For example, as an open learning course, as a reference resource, as a training resource, etc.

....

How did you hear about the Institue of Management Open Learning Programme?:

Word of mouth: Through my tutor/trainer: Mailshot:

Other (please give details):...

Many thanks for your help in returning this form.

Institute of Management Open Learning Programme

This programme comprises seventeen workbooks, each on a core management topic with the latest management thinking, as well as a *User Guide* and a *Mentor Guide*.

Designed for self study through open learning, the workbooks cover all management experience from team building to budgeting, from the skills of self management to manage strategically for organizational success.

TITLE	ISBN	Price
The Influential Manager	0 7506 3662 9	£22.50
Managing Yourself	0 7506 3661 0	£22.50
Getting the Right People to Do the Right Job	0 7506 3660 2	£22.50
Understanding Business Process Management	0 7506 3659 9	£22.50
Customer Focus	0 7506 3663 7	£22.50
Getting TQM to Work	0 7506 3664 5	£22.50
Leading from the Front	0 7506 3665 3	£22.50
Improving Your Organization's Success	0 7506 3666 1	£22.50
Project Management	0 7506 3667 X	£22.50
Budgeting and Financial Control	0 7506 3668 8	£22.50
Effective Financial and Resource Management	0 7506 3669 6	£22.50
Developing Yourself and Your Staff	0 7506 3670 X	£22.50
Building a High Performance Team	0 7506 3671 8	£22.50
The New Model Leader	0 7506 3672 6	£22.50
Making Rational Decisions	0 7506 3673 4	£22.50
Communication	0 7506 3674 2	£22.50
Successful Information Management	0 7506 3675 0	£22.50
User Guide	0 7506 3676 9	£22.50
Mentor Guide	0 7506 3677 7	£22.50
Full set of workbooks plus *Mentor Guide* and *User Guide*	0 7506 3359 X	£370.00

To order: *(Please quote ISBNs when ordering)*

- College Orders: 01865 314333
- Account holders: 01865 314301
- Individual Purchases: 01865 314627

(Please have credit card details ready)

For further information or to request a full series brochure, please contact:

Tessa Gingell on 01865 314477